Contents

Historical Chart

This chart covers the most important periods of British history. It shows the chief inhabitants or invaders of England until the Middle Ages, then the royal houses of England (until 1603) and of Britain (after 1603). Only monarchs or rulers mentioned in the text appear on the chart.

The Celts	900 B.C.–55 B.C.	
The Romans	55 B.C.–450 A.D.	
The Anglo-Saxons	450–1066	Offa (8th century)
The Viking Invaders	8th–11th centuries	
The Normans	1066–1154	William the Conqueror (1066–1087)
The Plantagenets	1154–1399	Henry II (1154–1189) Edward I (1212–1307)
The Houses of York and Lancaster	1399–1485	
The Tudors	1485–1603	Henry VII (1484–1509) Henry VIII (1509–1547) Mary I ('Bloody Mary') (1553–1558) Elizabeth I (1558–1603)
The Stuarts (The Civil War	1603–1649 1628–1649)	James I (1603–1625) Charles I (1625–1649)
The Republic	1649–1660	Oliver Cromwell (1649–1660)
The Stuarts	1660–1714	William and Mary (1688–1702)
The Hanoverians	1714–1901	George I, II, III, IV (1714–1830) ('Georgian' period) Victoria (1837–1901) ('Victorian' period)
The House of Saxe-Coburg	1901–1910	Edward VII (1901–1910) ('Edwardian' period)
The House of Windsor	1910–	Elizabeth II (1952–)

The Middle Ages { The Plantagenets ... The Houses of York and Lancaster

1 The United Kingdom

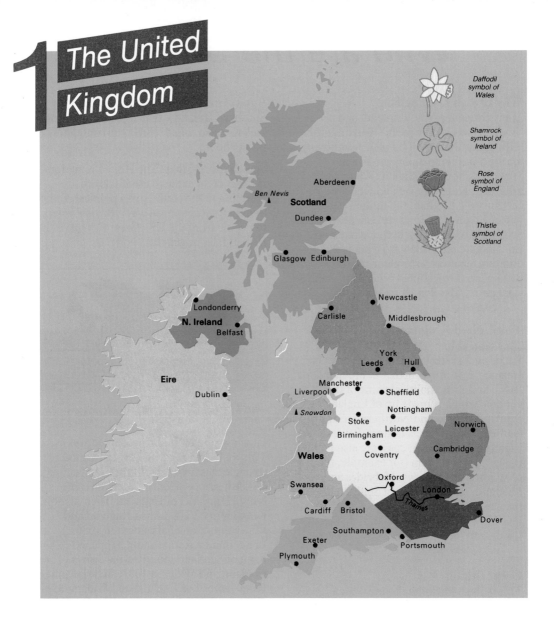

Daffodil symbol of Wales

Shamrock symbol of Ireland

Rose symbol of England

Thistle symbol of Scotland

Aberdeen

Ben Nevis

Scotland

Dundee

Glasgow Edinburgh

Newcastle

Londonderry

Carlisle

Middlesbrough

N. Ireland

Belfast

York

Leeds Hull

Eire

Manchester

Dublin

Liverpool Sheffield

Snowdon Nottingham

Stoke

Norwich

Leicester

Birmingham

Cambridge

Wales Coventry

Oxford

Swansea London

Thames

Cardiff Bristol

Dover

Southampton

Exeter Portsmouth

Plymouth

The United Kingdom is very small compared with many other countries in the world. However, there are only nine other countries with more people, and London is the world's seventh biggest city.

The main areas of high land are in Scotland, Wales and Cumbria. In the centre of England is a range of hills called the Pennines, which are also known as the 'backbone of England'. The highest mountains are in Scotland and Wales: Ben Nevis is 4,406 feet (1,343 m.) and Snowdon is 3,560 feet (1,085 m.). Of course, these are very small compared with other mountains in the world – Everest, the highest mountain in the world, is 29,000 feet (8,839 m.). In fact everything in the United Kingdom is rather small – the longest rivers are the Severn (220 miles, 354 km.) and the River Thames (215 miles, 346 km.). Compare these with the River Amazon in South America which is 4,195 miles (6,751 km.) long!

Despite its size, there is a great deal of variety within the islands of the United Kingdom, and this book aims to show the particular character of each country and region.

Who are the British?

Why British not English?

Many foreigners say 'England' and 'English' when they mean 'Britain', or the 'UK', and 'British'. This is very annoying for the 5 million people who live in Scotland, the 2.8 million in Wales and 1.5 million in Northern Ireland who are certainly *not* English. (46 million people live in England.) However, the people from Scotland, Wales, Northern Ireland and England are all British. So what is the difference between the names 'Great Britain' and 'the United Kingdom' – and what about 'the British Isles'?

The United Kingdom

This is an abbreviation of 'the United Kingdom of Great Britain and Northern Ireland'. It is often further abbreviated to 'UK', and is the political name of the country which is made up of England, Scotland, Wales and Northern Ireland (sometimes known as Ulster). Several islands off the British coast are also part of the United Kingdom (for example, the Isle of Wight, the Orkneys, Hebrides and Shetlands, and the Isles of Scilly), although the Channel Islands and the Isle of Man are not. However, all these islands do recognize the Queen.

Great Britain

This is the name of the island which is made up of England, Scotland and Wales and so, strictly speaking, it does not include Northern Ireland. The origin of the word 'Great' is a reference to size, because in many European languages the words for Britain and Brittany in France are the same. In fact, it was the French who first talked about *Grande Bretagne*! In everyday speech 'Britain' is used to mean the United Kingdom.

The British Isles

This is the geographical name that refers to all the islands off the north west coast of the European continent: Great Britain, the whole of Ireland (Northern and Southern), the Channel Islands and the Isle of Man.

But it is important to remember that Southern Ireland – that is the Republic of Ireland (also called 'Eire') – is completely independent.

So you can see that 'The United Kingdom' is the correct name to use if you are referring to the country in a political, rather than in a geographical way. 'British' refers to people from the UK, Great Britain or the British Isles in general.

The Welsh flag, called the Welsh dragon.

How was the United Kingdom formed? This took centuries, and a lot of armed struggle was involved. In the 15th century, a Welsh prince, Henry Tudor, became King Henry VII of England. Then his son, King Henry VIII, united England and Wales under one Parliament in 1536. In Scotland a similar thing happened. The King of Scotland inherited the crown of England and Wales in 1603, so he became King James I of England and Wales and King James VI of Scotland. The Parliaments of England, Wales and Scotland were united a century later in 1707.

The Scottish and Welsh are proud and independent people. In recent years there have been attempts at devolution in the two countries, particularly in Scotland where the Scottish Nationalist Party was very strong for a while. However, in a referendum in 1978 the Welsh rejected devolution and in 1979 the Scots did the same. So it seems that most Welsh and Scottish people are happy to form part of the UK even though they sometimes complain that they are dominated by England, and particularly by London.

The whole of Ireland was united with Great Britain from 1801 up until 1922. In that year the independent Republic of Ireland was formed in the South, while Northern Ireland became part of the United Kingdom of Great Britain and Northern Ireland. The story of this particular union is long and complicated and you will read more about it in Unit 10.

The Union Jack

The flag of the United Kingdom, known as the Union Jack, is made up of three crosses. The upright red cross is the cross of St George, the patron saint of England. The white diagonal cross (with the arms going into the corners) is the cross of St Andrew, the patron saint of Scotland. The red diagonal cross is the cross of St Patrick, the patron saint of Ireland. St David is the patron saint of Wales.

Invasion

What makes the Scottish, Welsh, English and Northern Irish different from each other? About 2,000 years ago the British Isles were inhabited by the Celts who originally came from continental Europe. During the next 1,000 years there were many invasions. The Romans came from Italy in AD 43 and, in calling the country 'Britannia', gave Britain its name. The Angles and Saxons came from Germany, Denmark and the Netherlands in the 5th century, and England gets its name from this invasion (Angle-land). The Vikings arrived from Denmark and Norway throughout the 9th century, and in 1066 (the one date in history which every British school-child knows) the Normans invaded

from France. These invasions drove the Celts into what is now Wales and Scotland, and they remained, of course, in Ireland. The English, on the other hand, are the descendants of all the invaders, but are more Anglo-Saxon than anything else. These various origins explain many of the differences to be found between England, Wales, Scotland and Ireland – differences in education, religion and the legal systems, but most obviously, in language.

Language

The Celts spoke Celtic which survives today in the form of Welsh, Scottish Gaelic and Irish Gaelic. Less than a quarter of all Welsh people (600,000, out of 2,800,000) speak Welsh. Scottish Gaelic and Irish Gaelic are still spoken, although they have suffered more than Welsh from the spread of English. However, all three languages are now officially encouraged and taught in schools.

English developed from Anglo-Saxon and is a Germanic language. However, all the invading peoples, particularly the Norman French, influenced the English language and you can find many words in English which are French in origin. Nowadays all Welsh, Scottish and Irish people speak English (even if they speak their own language as well), but all the countries have their own special accents and dialects, and their people are easily recognizable as soon as they speak. Occasionally, people from the four countries in the UK have difficulty in understanding one another because of these different accents. A southern English accent is generally accepted to be the most easily understood, and is the accent usually taught to foreigners.

Multiracial Britain

Recently, there have been many waves of immigration into Britain and movement within the UK. For example, many people from Wales, Scotland and Ireland have settled in England; and Jews, Russians, Germans, and Poles have come to Britain (particularly London) during political changes in the rest of Europe.

Commonwealth citizens were allowed free entry into Britain until 1962. Before the Second World War these immigrants were mostly people from Canada, Australia, New Zealand and South Africa. In the 1950s, people from the West Indies, India, Pakistan, Bangladesh and Hong Kong were encouraged to come and work in Britain. Today, 2 million British people are of West Indian or Asian origin and over 50 per cent of them were born in Britain.

The new immigrant communities are concentrated in the following towns and cities: London, Slough, Leicester, Wolverhampton, Birmingham, Luton, Bradford, Coventry, Bedford, Reading and Sandwell. The main languages of the Asian immigrants are Urdu, Hindi, Bengali, Punjabi, Gujarati, and Cantonese (Chinese). Nowadays the policy is to encourage these communities to continue speaking their own languages as well as English. The children of immigrants are often taught their own languages in school, and there are special newspapers, magazines, and radio and television programmes for the Asian community. The West Indians, of course, arrive speaking English, but they do have their own culture which they wish to keep alive. They also have their own newspapers, and radio and television programmes.

This latest wave of immigration has of course caused problems. There is certainly racial tension and racial prejudice in Britain today. In spite of laws passed to protect them, there is still discrimination against Asian and black people, many of whom are unemployed or in low-paid jobs. However, the atmosphere is improving and the different races are slowly learning to trust one another. In a wide educational programme white school-children, teachers, policemen and social workers are learning about the problems and customs of their new neighbours. There are many areas in Britain now where racial harmony is a reality.

British culture is being enriched through its contact with other cultures. For example, the British are becoming more adventurous in their cooking and eating habits, and Chinese, Indian and Pakistani restaurants are very popular. Another example can be found in the pop music scene where West Indian reggae music has become very influential.

WORDS

The English come from England, the Scots from Scotland, the Welsh from Wales and the Irish from Ireland. Think of as many European countries as you can. What are the people called? What language do they speak?

TALKING POINTS

- What invasions has your country suffered in the past 2,000 years? What effects have these invasions had?
- Are there any immigrants in your country? Have there been any problems associated with immigrants? If so, what should be done to solve these problems?
- Do many people from your country go to live and work in other countries? Are they treated well?

The political system

The United Kingdom is a constitutional monarchy. This means that it has a monarch (a king or a queen) as its Head of State. The monarch has very little power and can only reign with the support of Parliament. Parliament consists of two chambers known as the House of Commons and the House of Lords. Parliament and the monarch have different roles in the government of the country, and they only meet together on symbolic occasions such as the coronation of a new monarch or the opening of Parliament. In reality, the House of Commons is the only one of the three which has true power. It is here that new bills are introduced and debated. If the majority of the members are in favour of a bill it goes to the House of Lords to be debated and finally to the monarch to be signed. Only then does it become law. Although a bill must be supported by all three bodies, the House of Lords only has limited powers, and the monarch has not refused to sign one since the modern political system began over 200 years ago.

The House of Commons and the electoral system

The House of Commons is made up of 650 elected members, known as Members of Parliament (abbreviated to MPs), each of whom represents an area (or constituency) of the United Kingdom. They are elected either at a general election, or at a by-election following the death or retirement of an MP. The election campaign usually lasts about three weeks. Everyone over the age of 18 can vote in an election, which is decided on a simple majority – the candidate with the most votes wins. Under this system, an MP who wins by a small number of votes may have more votes against him (that is, for the other candidates) than for him. This is a very simple system, but many people think that it is unfair because the wishes of those who voted for the unsuccessful candidates are not represented at all. Parliamentary elections must be held every five years at the latest, but the Prime Minister can decide on the exact date within those five years.

Voting figures for the 1987 election			
Party	Percentage of total vote	Number of MPs	Percentage of MPs
Conservative	42%	375	58%
Labour	31%	229	35%
Liberal SDP Alliance	23%	22	3%

The party system

The British democratic system depends on political parties, and there has been a party system of some kind since the 17th century. The political parties choose candidates in elections (there are sometimes independent candidates, but they are rarely elected). The party which wins the majority of seats forms the Government and its leader usually becomes Prime Minister. The largest minority party becomes the Opposition. In doing so it accepts the right of the majority party to run the country, while the majority party accepts the right of the minority party to criticize it. Without this agreement between the political parties, the British parliamentary system would break down.

The Prime Minister chooses about twenty MPs from his or her party to become Cabinet Ministers. Each minister is responsible for a particular area of government, and for a Civil Service department. For example, the Minister of Defence is responsible for defence policy and the armed forces, the Chancellor of the Exchequer for financial policy, and the Home Secretary for, among other things, law and order and immigration. Their Civil

Service departments are called the Ministry of Defence, the Treasury and the Home Office respectively. They are staffed by civil servants who are politically neutral and who therefore do not change if the Government changes. The leader of the Opposition also chooses MPs to take responsibility for opposing the Government in these areas. They are known as the 'Shadow Cabinet'.

The parliamentary parties

The Conservative and Liberal parties are the oldest, and until the last years of the 19th century they were the only parties elected to the House of Commons. Once working-class men were given the vote, however, Socialist MPs were elected, but it was not until 1945 that Britain had its first Labour Government. At this election, the number of Liberal MPs was greatly reduced and since then Governments have been formed by either the Labour or the Conservative party. Usually they have had clear majorities – that is, one party has had more MPs than all the others combined.

The Conservative Party can broadly be described as the party of the middle and upper classes although it does receive some working-class support. Most of its voters live in rural areas, small towns and the suburbs of large cities. Much of its financial support comes from large industrial companies. The Labour Party, on the other hand, has always had strong links with the trade unions and receives financial support from them. While many Labour voters are middle-class or intellectuals, the traditional Labour Party support is still strongest in industrial areas.

In 1981, some MPs left the Labour Party to form a new 'left-of-centre' party – the Social Democratic Party (SDP) – which they hoped would win enough support to break the two-party system of the previous forty years. They fought the 1983 election in an alliance with the Liberals, but only a small number of their MPs were elected. In 1988, the majority of SDP and Liberal MPs and party members decided to form a permanent single party, to be called the Social, Democratic and Liberal Party or The Social and Liberal Democrats. However, some SDP MPs and party members disagreed with the idea, and so the SDP still exists as a separate party. They (and other small minority parties in the House of Commons) would like to change the electoral system; they want MPs to be elected by proportional representation. Under this system, the number of MPs from each party would correspond to the total number of votes each party receives in the election. The table on page 5 shows clearly why the Social, Democratic and Liberal Party thinks the present system is unfair.

1 *The Speaker's chair – he keeps order during debates.*
2 *The Government sit here. Cabinet Ministers sit on the Front Bench.*
3 *The Opposition sit on this side. The Shadow Cabinet face the Cabinet.*
4 *Other MPs sit here according to their party.*

The debating chamber of the House of Commons.

The House of Lords

The House of Lords has more than 1,000 members, although only about 250 take an active part in the work of the House. There are 26 Anglican bishops, 950 hereditary peers, 11 judges and 185 life peers, and unlike MPs they do not receive a salary. They debate a bill after it has been passed by the House of Commons. Changes may be recommended, and agreement between the two Houses is reached by negotiation. The Lords' main power consists of being able to delay non-financial bills for a period of a year, but they can also introduce certain types of bill. The House of Lords is the only non-elected second chamber among all the democracies in the world, and some people in Britain would like to abolish it.

The monarchy

The powers of the monarch are not defined precisely. Theoretically every act of government is done in the Queen's name – every letter sent out by a government department is marked 'On Her Majesty's Service' – and she appoints all the Ministers, including the Prime Minister. In reality, everything is done on the advice of the elected Government, and the monarch takes no part in the decision-making process.

Local government

Parliament in London is responsible for deciding national policy, but many public services are provided by local government. The United Kingdom is divided into administrative areas known as 'counties' and each county has a 'county town' where the offices of the local government are located. Local government is responsible for organising such services as education, libraries, police and fire services, road-building and many others.

TALKING POINT

Some people think that the monarchy should be abolished because it has no power and it costs the State a lot of money to maintain. How useful do you think the monarchy is in Britain today?

Religion

Throughout British history religion has been closely connected with kings, queens and politics. England was a Roman Catholic country until 1534. Why did this change?

When a king and a pope quarrelled . . .
In 1525 King Henry VIII decided to divorce his queen, Catherine of Aragon who, at the age of forty, was five years older than Henry. Also, she had only given him a daughter, and Henry wanted a son. He fell in love with Anne Boleyn who was younger, but when Henry asked the Pope for permission to divorce Catherine, he refused. Henry was so angry with the Pope that he ended all contact between England and Rome, divorced Catherine of Aragon without the Pope's permission and married Anne Boleyn. In 1534 Parliament named Henry head of the Church of England. This was the beginning of the Anglican Church. This quarrel with Rome was political, not religious. The Anglican Church did not start as a Protestant Church and Henry certainly did not regard himself as a Protestant. In fact, the Pope had given Henry the title of 'Defender of the Faith' in 1521 for words he wrote attacking Martin Luther, the German Protestant. (British kings and queens still have this title, and you can see the letters FID DEF or F.D. on British coins today.) However the Protestant movement in Europe was growing very strong at this time. When Henry quarrelled with Rome and ordered the Bible to be translated into English, the way was open for Protestantism to spread in England. Over the next years many people changed to this new religion.

*1 **Catherine of Aragon** – divorced.*

*2 **Anne Boleyn** – executed.*

*3 **Jane Seymour** – died in childbirth.*

Changing wives became a habit with Henry. Altogether he had six!

*4 **Anne of Cleves** – divorced.*

*5 **Catherine Howard** –★ executed.*

*6 **Catherine Parr** – lived longer than Henry.*

In 1553 Mary, Henry's daughter by Catherine of Aragon, became Queen of England. Because she was a Roman Catholic, the country re-entered the Roman Church. While Mary was Queen, many Protestants were burned at the stake for their beliefs. She also put her non-Roman Catholic sister, Elizabeth (the daughter of Henry and Anne Boleyn), into prison in the Tower of London. Protestants were glad when Mary died in 1558 and Elizabeth became Queen. Elizabeth also became head of the Anglican Church, like her father, and Roman Catholicism was never again the established (official) religion in England.

The Puritans

After Elizabeth became Queen, a group of Protestants wanted to 'purify' the Church of England of all Roman Catholic influence. These people were called Puritans – they were the English Protestants. They dressed very simply and believed that all pleasures, such as fine clothes and the theatre, were wicked.

When James I was King (1603–1625) the Puritans were often put in prison and sometimes even killed. Some of them decided to leave England to find freedom in a new country.

They sailed from Plymouth in 1620 in a ship called the 'Mayflower', and these 'Pilgrim Fathers' – as they were called – started a new life in America. The service which they held to thank God for their arrival, became a traditional annual festival in America, called 'Thanksgiving'.

Under the rule of James I's son, Charles I, the Puritans were treated even worse. Many people sympathized with the Puritans, and the Court was unpopular because it was suspected of being a centre of Roman Catholicism. (This was because Charles's

---

★There are no pictures of Catherine Howard. This was once thought to be her.

wife was a Roman Catholic.) This religious split between the Puritans and the Court was one cause of the outbreak of civil war in 1628 and the eventual execution of Charles I. Following this, from 1649 to 1660, Britain was a republic for a short while.

Religion today

The Church of England – or the Anglican Church – is still the established church in England, and the British king or queen is still head of the Church. There are, however, many other churches to which people belong: for example Roman Catholics (6 million) and the basically protestant Methodists (1,150,000), Congregationalists (372,000), Baptists (338,000) and other smaller groups. The Methodists and Baptists are particularly strong in Wales.

A friendly Church of England vicar greets one of his parishioners.

In Scotland the Presbyterian Church (called the *kirk*) is the established church and it is completely separate from the Church of England. The Presbyterian Church is based on a strict form of Protestantism which was taught by the French reformer, Calvin, and brought to Scotland by John Knox.

Although there is complete religious freedom in Britain today, there is still tension between Catholics and Protestants in Northern Ireland, where religion is still caught up with politics (see Unit 10).

Britain's immigrants have also brought with them their own religions which they continue to practise. There are Muslims, Hindus and Sikhs from the Indian subcontinent, Rastafarians from the West Indies, and the largest group of Jews living in Europe.

Rastafarian men often wear their hair in dreadlocks.

In spite of the great variety of forms of worship, only a minority of people regularly go to church in Britain today. Most people see Sunday more as a day for relaxing with the family or for doing jobs around the house and the garden.

Family life

A 'typical' British family used to consist of mother, father and two children, but in recent years there have been many changes in family life. Some of these have been caused by new laws and others are the result of changes in society. For example, since the law made it easier to get a divorce, the number of divorces has increased. In fact one marriage in every three now ends in divorce. This means that there are a lot of one-parent families. Society is now more tolerant than it used to be of unmarried people, unmarried couples and single parents.

Another change has been caused by the fact that people are living longer nowadays, and many old people live alone following the death of their partners. As a result of these changes in the pattern of people's lives, there are many households which consist of only one person or one adult and children.

You might think that marriage and the family are not so popular as they once were. However, the majority of divorced people marry again, and they sometimes take responsibility for a second family.

Members of a family – grandparents, aunts, uncles, cousins – keep in touch, but they see less of each other than they used to. This is because people often move away from their home town to work, and so the family becomes scattered. Christmas is the traditional season for reunions. Although the family group is smaller nowadays than it used to be, relatives often travel many miles in order to spend the holiday together.

In general, each generation is keen to become independent of parents in establishing its own family unit, and this fact can lead to social as well as geographical differences within the larger family group.

Who looks after the older generation?
There are about 10 million old-age pensioners in Britain, of whom about 750,000 cannot live entirely independently. The government gives financial help in the form of a pension but in the future it will be more and more difficult for the national economy to support the increasing number of elderly. At the present time, more than half of all old people are looked after at home. Many others live in Old Peoples' Homes, which may be private or state-owned.

The individual and the family
Relationships within the family are different now. Parents treat their children more as equals than they used to, and children have more freedom to make their own decisions. The father is more involved with bringing up children, often because the mother goes out to work. Increased leisure facilities and more money mean that there are greater opportunities for the individual to take part in activities outside the home. Although the family holiday is still an important part of family life (usually taken in August, and often abroad) many children have holidays away from their parents, often with a school party or other organized group.

TALKING POINT

People say that children today grow up more quickly. The law sometimes makes this possible. Look at the information below – how is the law different in your country?

> **YOUNG PEOPLE AND THE LAW**
>
> **Age 13** may be employed part-time.
> **Age 14** allowed in bars but not to drink alcohol.
> **Age 15** legally a 'young person' and not a 'child'.
> **Age 16** school leaving age, can leave home, drive a moped, marry with parents' consent (not needed in Scotland), buy beer with a meal.
> **Age 17** can drive a car or motorbike.
> **Age 18** age of majority – can vote, get married without parents' consent, own property, get tattooed, drink in pubs . . .

Festivals

On New Year's Eve, people traditionally take a shower in the fountains in Trafalgar Square! The Christmas tree is an annual gift from Norway

I'm in love!
On 14th February, St Valentine's Day, many people send a card to the one they love or someone whom they have fallen in love with. People usually do not sign these cards and a lot of time is spent trying to guess who has sent them!

Pancake Day
Ash Wednesday is the day in February when the Christian period of Lent begins. This refers to the time when Christ went into the desert and fasted for forty days. Although not many people actually give up eating during this period, on Pancake Tuesday, the day before Ash Wednesday, they eat lots of pancakes. These are made from flour, milk and eggs, and fried in a hot pan.

Some towns also hold pancake races on that day. People run through the streets holding a frying pan and throwing the pancake in the air. Of course if they drop the pancake they lose the race!

Easter eggs
At Easter time, the British celebrate the idea of new birth by giving each other chocolate Easter eggs which are opened and eaten on Easter Sunday. On Good Friday bakers sell hot cross buns, which are toasted and eaten with butter. Easter Monday is a holiday and many people travel to the seaside for the day or go and watch one of the many sporting events, such as football or horse-racing.

May is here

As summer comes, Britain likes to celebrate the end of the winter. In England on 1st May, Morris men may be seen in country areas celebrating traditional dances, waving their white handkerchiefs to drive away the evil spirits and welcome in the new ones. At school and in smaller village communities children may dance traditional spring dances such as the Maypole, when they weave their brightly coloured scarves into a beautiful pattern around a long pole.

Ghosts and witches

Hallowe'en means 'holy evening', and takes place on 31st October. Although it is a much more important festival in the United States than Britain, it is celebrated by many people in the UK. It is particularly connected with witches and ghosts.

At parties people dress up in strange costumes and pretend they are witches. They cut horrible faces in potatoes and other vegetables and put a candle inside, which shines through the eyes. People may play difficult games such as trying to eat an apple from a bucket of water without using their hands.

In recent years children dressed in white sheets knock on doors at Hallowe'en and ask if you would like a 'trick' or 'treat'. If you give them something nice, a 'treat', they go away. However, if you don't they play a 'trick' on you, such as making a lot of noise or spilling flour on your front doorstep!

Guy Fawkes Night

In 1605 King James I was on the throne. As a Protestant, he was very unpopular with Roman Catholics. Some of them planned to blow up the Houses of Parliament on 5th November of that year, when the King was going to open Parliament. Under the House of Lords they had stored thirty-six barrels of gun powder, which were to be exploded by a man called Guy Fawkes. However one of the plotters spoke about these plans and Fawkes was discovered, arrested and later hanged. Since that day the British traditionally celebrate 5th November by burning a dummy, made of straw and old clothes, on a bonfire, whilst at the same time letting off fireworks.

This dummy is called a 'guy' (like Guy Fawkes) and children can often be seen on the pavements before 5th November saying, 'Penny for the guy.' If they collect enough money they can buy some fireworks.

There are a lot of traditions connected with Christmas but perhaps the most important one is the giving of presents. Family members wrap up their gifts and leave them at the bottom of the Christmas tree to be found on Christmas morning. Children leave a long sock or stocking at the end of their bed on Christmas Eve, 24th December, hoping that Father Christmas will come down the chimney during the night and bring them small presents, fruit and nuts. They are usually not disappointed! At some time on Christmas Day the family will sit down to a big turkey dinner followed by Christmas pudding. They will probably pull a cracker with another member of the family. It will make a loud crack and a coloured hat, small toy and joke will fall out!

Later in the afternoon they may watch the Queen on television as she delivers her traditional Christmas message to the United Kingdom and the Commonwealth. If they have room for even more food they may enjoy a piece of Christmas cake or eat a hot mince pie. 26th December is also a public holiday, Boxing Day, and this is the time to visit friends and relatives or be a spectator at one of the many sporting events.

Christmas

If you try to catch a train on 24th December you may have difficulty in finding a seat. This is the day when many people are travelling home to be with their families on Christmas Day, 25th December. For most British families, this is the most important festival of the year, it combines the Christian celebration of the birth of Christ with the traditional festivities of winter.

On the Sunday before Christmas many churches hold a carol service where special hymns are sung. Sometimes carol-singers can be heard on the streets as they collect money for charity. Most families decorate their houses with brightly-coloured paper or holly, and they usually have a Christmas tree in the corner of the front room, glittering with coloured lights and decorations.

QUIZ

1 Who was the mother of Queen Elizabeth I?
2 From which group of invaders did England gets its name?
3 What happens to a bill after it has been passed by the House of Commons?
4 Where would you find a kirk?
5 What do families usually give each other on Easter Sunday?
6 What is the name of Britain's highest mountain?
7 Name two areas in Britain where a lot of immigrants live.
8 What is the connection between the 'Mayflower' and the United States of America?
9 At what age can you drive a car in Britain?
10 What is the maximum length of a Parliament?
11 What happens on St Valentine's Day?
12 Describe two of the three flags which make up the Union Jack.
13 Which country is sometimes called Ulster?
14 When do the British open their Christmas presents?
15 Why do some MPs want to change the electoral system?
16 A red dragon is the symbol of which country?

(You will find the answers on page 138.)

A FESTIVAL CROSSWORD

Across

1 You may see them at Hallowe'en.
5 'Trick . . . treat'.
6 . . . James I.
9 You can't buy much with this.
10 Send a card on Valentine's Day if you are . . . love.
11 The eleventh month.

Down

2 A lot of people go there at Christmas.
3 The English eat it on Christmas Day.
4 Would you like to . . . some carols?
7 Fireworks make a lot of this!
8 People dance . . . May 1st.
9 You cook pancakes in this.

(You will find the answers on page 138.)

Glossary

abbreviate to make short
abolish to end
Anglican of the Church of England
annoying causing anger or irritation
appoint to choose
armed struggle fighting with weapons
bill the special name for a proposal before it becomes law

blow up to explode
break down (*v*) not to work
broadly approximately
bun a sweet bread roll
carol a Christmas hymn
caught up with involved with
the Civil Service government administration

the Commonwealth an organization of independent states which were part of the British empire

continental Europe the part of Europe that excludes the British Isles

coronation a ceremony when a new monarch is crowned

correspond to to represent

criticize to find faults with

cruelty pleasure in causing pain

debate (*v*) to discuss formally

devolution giving part of the power of government to a smaller area or country

diagonal a line going from one corner of a rectangle to the opposite corner

discrimination treating someone differently because of their colour, race, religion or sex

dragon a mythical animal

dreadlocks long strands of tightly-curled hair – a style typical of Rastafarian men

dummy an object made to look like a real person

elderly old (people)

election campaign an organized attempt to persuade people to vote for a particular political party

enrich make richer or more interesting

evil bad

execute to kill

the Faith Christianity

fast (*v*) to stop eating

festivity a celebration

ghost a spirit

glitter to shine

hanged killed by hanging from a rope tied round the neck

harmful causing harm or injury

hereditary peer a lord who has gained his title by birth

Hindu a member of an Indian religion

holly a plant with prickly leaves

hymn a song sung in Church

immigrate to come and live in a new country

life peer a lord whose title will not be inherited by his children

maintain to keep

mince-pie a small pie filled with dried fruit and spices

moped a motorized bicycle

Morris men traditional dancers

multiracial having many races

Muslim a member of the Islamic religion

negotiation discussion

neutral not belonging to any one party

old-age pensioner a woman over 60 or a man over 65, receiving a state pension

outbreak (*n*) the start

patron saint a saint who is strongly associated with a particular country

political party a group of people united in politics

prejudice (*n*) thinking badly of people without really knowing them

Protestantism a form of Christianity started by Martin Luther in the 16th century, when he 'protested' against Roman Catholicism

public holiday a day when nobody goes to work

range a line

Rastafarian a member of a West Indian religion

referendum a vote 'yes' or 'no' on one question only

reggae West Indian pop music with a strong rhythm

reign (*v*) (of a monarch) to rule

reunion a meeting, usually after a long period of separation

rural of or in the country

scattered in different places

Sikh a member of an Indian religion

social worker a person employed to give help or advice

staff (*v*) to supply an institution (e.g. a school or a department) with workers

stake (*n*) a piece of wood to which people were tied to be killed, especially by burning

suburb an area on the edge of a city

tattoo (*v*) to mark skin with words or pictures

tolerant accepting (different ideas or people)

in touch in contact

trade union an organization of a group of workers

turkey a big bird

wave (*n*) a period

wicked bad

witch a woman who uses magic

working class people who work, for example, in factories (contrast upper class and middle class)

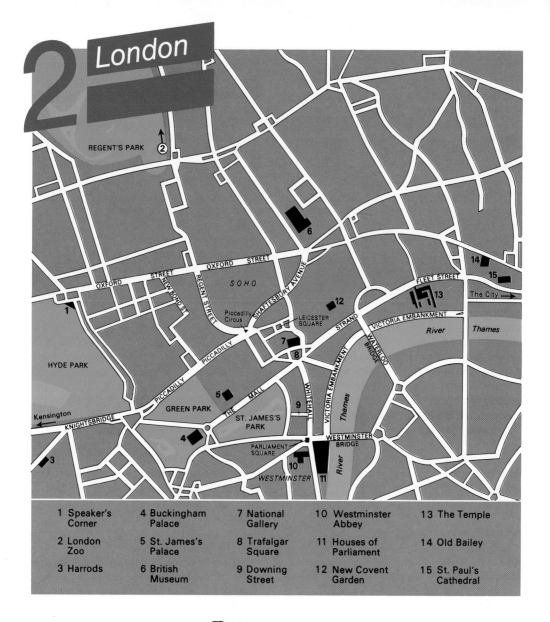

London

REGENT'S PARK ②

6

OXFORD STREET

OXFORD STREET
NEW BOND S.
REGENT STREET

SOHO

SHAFTESBURY AVENUE

14
15
FLEET STREET

Piccadilly
Circus
LEICESTER
SQUARE

13
12

The City →

STRAND

VICTORIA EMBANKMENT

River   Thames

1

7
8

PICCADILLY

HYDE PARK

VICTORIA EMBANKMENT

WATERLOO BRIDGE

5

THE MALL

9

Thames

Kensington

KNIGHTSBRIDGE

PICCADILLY

GREEN PARK

ST. JAMES'S
PARK

WHITEHALL

4

WESTMINSTER
BRIDGE

PARLIAMENT
SQUARE

3

10

River

11

WESTMINSTER

1 Speaker's Corner	4 Buckingham Palace	7 National Gallery	10 Westminster Abbey	13 The Temple
2 London Zoo	5 St. James's Palace	8 Trafalgar Square	11 Houses of Parliament	14 Old Bailey
3 Harrods	6 British Museum	9 Downing Street	12 New Covent Garden	15 St. Paul's Cathedral

London Regional Transport

The easiest way to travel around London is by a London Regional Transport bus or underground train. These run from the centre of the city right out into the countryside.

British people queue up when waiting for a bus (and lots of other things!). They get very annoyed with queue-jumpers – people who don't wait their turn in the queue.

The London Underground – or 'tube' – has nine lines. It's very fast, and in Central London you're never more than a few minutes' walk away from a station.

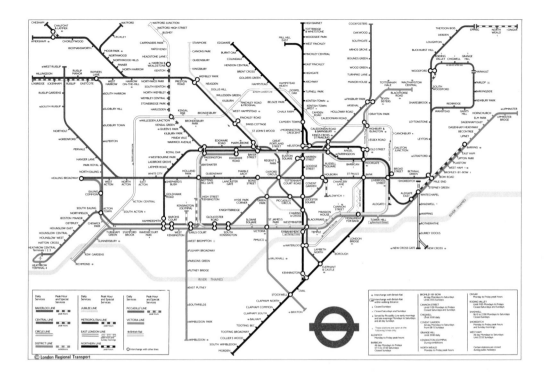

LOOK AND PRACTISE

Visitor Excuse me, please. Can you tell me how to get to Buckingham Palace?

Londoner Well, Euston station is just across the road, and Buckingham Palace is near St James's Park. So you'd better take the Northern Line going south. Then change at Embankment on to the Circle or District Line going west.

Visitor Thanks a lot!

You are at Piccadilly Circus. Using the maps above, choose a place to visit, and practise similar dialogues with a partner. Take it in turns to be the visitor.

ANSWER

1 What is the tube?
2 What must you do when waiting for a bus?
3 Would you prefer to travel in London by bus or by taxi or by tube? Why?

A city with a difference

London was not *built* as a city in the same way as Paris or New York. It began life as a Roman fortification at a place where it was possible to cross the River Thames. A wall was built around the town for defence, but during the long period of peace which followed the Norman Conquest, people built outside the walls. This building continued over the years, especially to the west of the city. In 1665 there was a terrible plague in London, so many people left the city and escaped to the villages in the surrounding countryside. In 1666 the Great Fire of London ended the plague, but it also destroyed much of the city. Although people returned to live in the rebuilt city after the plague and the Great Fire, there were never again so many Londoners living in the city centre.

These days not many people live in the city centre, but London has spread further outwards into the country, including surrounding villages. Today the metropolis of Greater London covers some 610 square miles (1580 sq. km.) and the suburbs of London continue even beyond this area. Some people even commute over 100 miles (over 150 km.) every day to work in

London, while living far away from the city in the country or in other towns.

The gradual growth of the city helps to explain the fact that London does not have just one centre, it has a number of centres, each with a distinct character: the financial and business centre called the City (spelt with a capital 'C'), the shopping and entertainment centre in the West End, the government centre in Westminster. Places like Highgate and Hampstead have kept their village-like character – they have their own newspapers and the famous Hampstead Heath is a reminder of country origins.

TALKING POINTS

- What do you know about the origins of the capital city of your country?
- Many people in Britain do not like living in city centres and so they commute to work from the suburbs and the surrounding countryside.
  What are the advantages and disadvantages of this?

The City

Tradition

The City does not refer to the whole of central London but rather to a small area east of the centre, which includes the site of the original Roman town. It is an area with a long and exciting history, and it is proud of its independence and traditional role as a centre of trade and commerce. This tradition is focussed on the City's Lord Mayor, whose official residence is the Mansion House. Once a year, in November, the Lord Mayor's Show takes place. This is a colourful street parade in which the newly elected Lord Mayor travels

in a golden coach, which is over 200 years old. In the evening a splendid meal is served in the Guildhall, to which the Prime Minister and members of the Government are invited.

Commerce and finance

The City of London is one of the major banking centres of the world and you can find the banks of many nations in the famous Threadneedle Street and the surrounding area. Here, too, you will find the Bank of England. Nearby is the Stock Exchange which is like a busy market, except that here not food but shares in commercial companies are bought and sold. A little further along in Leadenhall Street is Lloyds, the most famous insurance company in the world.

During weekdays in the City you can see the City gents with their bowler hats, pin-striped suits and rolled umbrellas. This is the 'uniform' only of those men involved in banking and business in the City, and outside this small area you will probably not see anyone dressed like this.

The Old Bailey

The centre of the country's judicial system is to be found in the western part of the City. The Old Bailey houses many courts and some of Britain's most famous murder trials have taken place here. Many solicitors and barristers have their offices (called 'chambers') nearby, particularly in the area known as the 'Temple'.

More uniforms! Barristers on their way to the courts at the Old Bailey.

All criminal trials in Britain are held before a judge and a jury consisting of twelve ordinary people. It is the jury, not the judge, who decides if a person is guilty or not. An accused person is considered innocent until proved guilty. All defendants are entitled to legal representation, which will be provided free if they cannot pay for it.

Quality Daily Newspapers
The Times, The Guardian, The Daily Telegraph, The Financial Times, The Independent.

Popular Daily Newspapers
The Daily Express, The Sun, The Mirror, The Daily Mail, Today, The Star.

Quality Sunday Newspapers
The Sunday Times, The Observer, The Sunday Telegraph.

Popular Sunday Newspapers
The News of the World, The People, The Mail on Sunday, The Sunday Mirror, The Sunday Express.

The press

Fleet Street is famous as the home of the nation's newspapers but, in fact, only two of them – *The Daily Express* and *The Daily Telegraph* – are still in Fleet Street. However, people still say 'Fleet Street' to mean 'the press'.

The British are a nation of newspaper readers. Many of them even have a daily paper delivered to their homes in time for breakfast!

British newspapers can be divided into two groups: quality and popular. Quality newspapers are more serious and cover home and foreign news thoughtfully while the popular newspapers like shocking, personal stories as well as some news. These two groups of papers can be distinguished easily because the quality newspapers are twice the size of the popular newspapers.

Historic buildings in the City

St Paul's Cathedral was designed by the famous architect Sir Christopher Wren, after the Great Fire of London in 1666. Prince Charles and Lady Diana Spencer were married there in July 1981.

The Tower of London was first built by William the Conqueror more than 900 years ago, and was famous as a prison. Two queens were executed here, and two princes murdered.

QUIZ

1 One influential daily newspaper in Britain is printed on pink paper. True or false?
2 One of the queens who was beheaded in the Tower was Catherine Howard. She was not the only wife to be beheaded. Who was the husband?
3 How do tall ships pass up the Thames beyond Tower Bridge?
4 What famous marriage took place at St Paul's Cathedral in July 1981?
5 What ancient London landmark was bought by an American, shipped stone by stone to the USA and rebuilt in Arizona?

(You will find the answers on page 138.)

The East End

The East End grew with the spread of industries to the east of the City, and the growth of the port of London. It covers a wide area. A part like Bethnal Green, which was once a country village, is quite different from the areas down by the river, where there are many wharfs and warehouses.

It is also one of those areas of London where people from abroad have come to find work. For centuries foreigners have made London their home. Some have had to leave their country for religious or political reasons. Others have wanted to find a better life. Some brought new skills and started new industries. These days, many Jews and Bengalis live in the East End, and within a small area you can see a mosque, a church and a synagogue! The East End is especially famous as the centre of the clothing industry (or 'rag-trade') in London.

The East End markets are famous throughout the world. Petticoat Lane market takes place every Sunday morning and has become one of the sights of London. Street-salesmen promise that the goods are of the highest quality and much cheaper than those you can buy in the West End! 'Come on darlin' . . . amazin' bargain

. . . you ain't seen nuffink like it!'

Traditionally someone born in the East End is known as a cockney although this name is now given to anyone who speaks like a Londoner. Typically they change certain vowel sounds so that the sound in 'late' becomes more like that in 'light'. In addition they don't use the usual 't' sound of standard English but stop the air in their throat. (Try saying 'bu'er' instead of 'butter'!) Like some foreign learners of English they seem to have a few problems with 'th' and use an 'f' instead!

During the last century, East End criminals developed a special kind of slang or language which made it difficult for the police to understand them. In certain parts of London this slang is still used, and some expressions have passed into normal, everyday English. It is called 'rhyming slang' because words are replaced by other words or phrases which rhyme. For example 'loaf of bread' means 'head', and 'butcher's hook' means 'look'. However, usually only the first word of the phrase is used, for example, 'Use your loaf!' means 'Use your head . . . don't be silly!' and 'Let me have a butcher's.' means 'Let me have a look.'

PUZZLE

Here are some examples of rhyming slang. Match the words on the right with the rhyming slang on the left.

Barnet Fair	Telephone
Bees and honey	Mouth
Daisy roots	Feet
Plates of meat	Hair
North and South	Money
Dog and bone	Boots

DOG AND BONE, GUV? RIGHT – TAKE A BUTCHER'S UP THE TOAD AND THEN USE YOUR MINCE PIES AND YOU'LL SEE IT.

(You will find the answers on page 138.)

The West End

The West End is the name given to the area of central London north from The Mall to Oxford Street. It includes Trafalgar Square, the main shopping areas of Oxford Street, Regent Street and Bond Street, and the entertainment centres of Soho, Piccadilly Circus, Leicester Square and Shaftesbury Avenue. Its name is associated with glamour and bright lights.

Trafalgar Square
Trafalgar Square was built early in the last century to commemorate the Battle of Trafalgar. Admiral Lord Nelson's statue stands on top of a column in the middle of Trafalgar Square. The square makes a good place for people to meet – coaches pick up parties of visitors, marchers unite for protest meetings, and at Christmas time carol singers gather round a huge Christmas tree which is sent to Britain from Norway every year. Behind Nelson's Column is the National Gallery, an art gallery in which you can find many old masters.

Shopping
Most of London's big department stores are in Oxford Street and Regent Street. They are always crowded, but at sale times, in . January and July, there are so many people that it is difficult to move and it is usually safer to go in the direction of the majority! These days, it is often difficult to distinguish the goods in one large store from those in another.

Trafalgar Square is a famous meeting place.

DO YOU KNOW?

A department store is a large shop which sells a wide range of goods in different departments, each with a special name. Here are some of them and beside them is a list of goods. In which department would you buy them? Look up the answer in your dictionary.

CONFECTIONERY
HARDWARE
ELECTRICAL
HABERDASHERY
STATIONERY
CAFETERIA
BEDDING

Sheets and pillowcases
a radio
chocolates
a cup of tea
a saucepan
a zip
a writing pad

Mrs Thatcher at Madame Tussaud's.

If you are looking for something 'different' (but cannot afford the prices of Bond Street) it is certainly worth going to New Covent Garden. This used to be England's biggest fruit and vegetable market, but a few years ago, the market was moved to a new site on the other side of the River Thames. The old market, now called 'New Covent Garden', was restored and converted into a shopping centre. There are now more than forty shops of many different kinds, and there are several places to eat and drink. The opening hours are different from most other shops: they open at 10 a.m. and close at 8 p.m., whereas most shops open from 9 a.m. to 5.30 p.m. As well as shopping, there is entertainment with lunch-time theatre groups and classical, jazz, folk and pop music.

Entertainment

Piccadilly Circus is the centre of night life in the West End. It is usually top of everyone's list of things to see in London, because it is so well known. It is actually quite small, and most people are rather disappointed when they see it for the first time because they had imagined it would be much bigger! To the north of Piccadilly Circus is Soho, which has been the foreign quarter of London since the 17th century. Now it has restaurants offering food from a variety of different countries, especially Chinese and Italian ones, as well as 'adult' entertainment.

London is famous for its live theatre, and there are over thirty theatres within a square mile. Naturally there is a great variety of shows to choose from: 'whodunnits', opera, musicals, drama, comedies and so on. If you want to know what is on in London, the best place to look is in a newspaper.

ACT IT OUT

Look at these advertisements.
Decide with a partner what you would like to see, then imagine that you have to telephone the theatre to book tickets. Plan what to say (decide on the price, day, performance, etc.) before acting out the dialogue with your partner.

NEW LONDON. CC Drury Lane WC2. 01-405 0072 or 01-404 4079 Evgs 7.45. Tue. & Sat. 3.0 & 7.45.
THE ANDREW LLOYD WEBBER T. S. ELIOT INTERNATIONAL AWARD WINNING MUSICAL

CATS

Group Bookings 01-405 1567 or 01-930 6123. Apply daily to Box Office for returns. LATECOMERS NOT ADMITTED WHILE AUDITORIUM IS IN MOTION. PLEASE BE PROMPT.
Bars open 6.45 p.m.
OVER 1,000 SOLD OUT PERFS

LONDON PALLADIUM. 01-437 7373. Evgs 7.30. Mats Wed & Sat 2.45.
FIRST EVER STAGE PRODUCTION
**TOMMY STEELE in
SINGIN'IN THE RAIN**
with ROY CASTLE

MAYFAIR. S. CC 629 3036. Mon.-Thurs. 8.0, Fri. & Sat. 5.40 & 8.10. Grp. 930 6123.
**RICHARD TODD
ERIC LANDER, VIRGINIA STRIDE** in
THE BUSINESS OF MURDER
"The best thriller for years." – S.
**THIRD GREAT YEAR
OVER 1,000 PERFORMANCES**

DUKE OF YORK'S. S CC 836 5122. CC only 836 0641. CC Hotline 930 9232. Mon. to Thurs. Evgs 8.0, Friday and Saturday 5.45 and 8.30.
**IAN OGILVY
ANGELA STEPHANIE
THORNE BEACHAM
JAMES LAURENSON in
HAPPY FAMILY**
By Giles Cooper
Directed by Maria Aitken

HAYMARKET THEATRE ROYAL. 930 9832. Group Sales 01-930 6123. Evgs 7.30. Mats Weds 2.30. Sats at 3.0. Reduced prices at Mat. for Senior Citizens.
**JOAN FRANK
PLOWRIGHT FINLAY
LESLIE PHILLIPS
JOANNA BILL FRANK
DAVID FRASER GRIMES
BERNARD MILES**
in
THE CHERRY ORCHARD
in **ANTON CHEKHOV**
Directed by **LINDSAY ANDERSON**
LIMITED SEASON ONLY

ST MARTIN'S. 836 1443. Special CC No 930 9232. Evgs 8.0. Tues. 2.45, Sats 5.0 and 8.0
AGATHA CHRISTIE'S
THE MOUSETRAP
31st Year
SORRY, no reduced prices from any source, but seats bookable from £3.

Westminster

Every day when people in the UK and overseas switch on their radio to listen to BBC radio news, they can hear one of the most famous sounds in London. On the hour, the bells of Big Ben ring loud and clear. Many people think that Big Ben is the clock or the whole tower next to the Houses of Parliament. In fact, it is the largest of the five bells at the top of the tower. Parliament itself is in Westminster, a part of London that has long been connected with royalty and government.

King Edward the Confessor first decided to build a palace beside the River Thames in the 11th century. His successors extended the palace and made it their main residence. Gradually, Westminster became the centre of government and justice. At first, Parliament was organized by the monarch as a way of governing the country. He or she called different groups together: the Lords represented the Church and aristocracy whilst the Commons were used by the rich land-owners to put forward the views and interests of their own town or village. Over the centuries power gradually passed from the monarch to Parliament but not without a few problems!

During the reign of James I, for example, Guy Fawkes tried to blow up Parliament (see page 12).

James' son, Charles I, thought that he could rule the country without the help of Parliament, but these dreams led to his death. He tried to make parliament do what he wanted, but after years of quarrelling he finally lost his patience. One day he burst into the House of Commons with several hundred men and tried to arrest its leaders. They had already escaped. But the struggle between king and parliament was not finished and the country was thrown into a civil war, which only stopped when Charles was finally beheaded in 1649.

The Queen still opens the new session of Parliament each autumn by reading 'the Queen's Speech', which describes the main policies of the Government. However, this takes place in the House of Lords and she is not allowed to enter the House of Commons. This tradition goes back to the time of Charles I, more than three hundred years ago, and reminds everybody that the monarch must not try to govern the country.

The Houses of Parliament were rebuilt in 1835 after being completely destroyed by fire. In addition, the House of Commons needed more repairs after being bombed during the Second World War. Parliament is in session every afternoon and evening except Friday and the weekend, and if you are lucky you might be able to watch a debate from the public gallery.

ASK

Ask questions for these answers.
1 Big Ben.
2 Guy Fawkes.
3 Charles I.
4 The Queen's Speech.
5 1835.

Westminster Abbey
Opposite the Houses of Parliament stands Westminster Abbey. A church has stood here since Saxon times when, in the year 750 AD, a Benedictine Abbey was founded. It was known as West Monastery (Westminster), from its position 3 miles (five kilometres) west of London's centre. From Norman times British monarchs have been crowned there and since the 13th century they have been buried there. Many other famous people are also buried in Westminster Abbey including statesmen, musicians and writers. In Poet's Corner can be found statues and the tombs of poets such as T.S. Eliot.

PRACTISE

Look at the photograph of Westminster and Whitehall opposite and describe the different buildings and where they are located. Give as much information as you can about each building or monument.

Whitehall

The street called Whitehall stretches from Parliament Square to Trafalgar Square. Just as Westminster or the Palace of Westminster frequently stands for the Houses of Parliament, so Whitehall is often used as a name for the Civil Service.

Downing Street, which is a small side street off Whitehall, is the home of the Prime Minister, who lives at number ten. Next door at number eleven lives the Chancellor of the Exchequer, who is responsible for financial planning and the British economy. Just around the corner in Whitehall itself are all the important ministries: the Foreign Office, the Ministry of Defence, the Home Office and the Treasury.

In the middle of Whitehall is the Cenotaph where the Queen lays the first wreath of poppies on Remembrance Day. On that day each year the people of Britain remember their dead from the two world wars of this century by wearing a red paper poppy.

HOW MUCH DO YOU REMEMBER?

Which ministers and ministries are responsible for the following areas of government?

Income tax	Law and order
The army	Nuclear weapons
Prisons	Immigration
Government spending	The police

(You will find the answers on page 138.)

Royal London

The Queen and her family on the balcony of Buckingham Palace.

You cannot go far in London without being aware of the city's close connection with the Crown. There are royal palaces, royal parks and colourful ceremonies; if you look at the souvenirs you can see how important royalty is to the capital's tourist industry.

The most important building, but not the most beautiful, is Buckingham Palace, which is the official residence of the Queen.

It overlooks St James's Park where the previous royal residence, St James's Palace, can be found. Running through the park, from Trafalgar Square to the front of Buckingham Palace is The Mall, a wide tree-lined avenue designed for royal processions on ceremonial occasions.

St James's Park is one of ten royal parks in and around London which are owned by the Crown but are open to the public free of charge. They make a special contribution to city-living because their existence has ensured that there are areas of green between the flats, office blocks and other buildings, and that there is somewhere quiet and attractive to escape to, away from traffic jams, crowded shops and congested pavements.

Each park has its own character. Hyde Park, for example, was originally a hunting forest and is still popular with horseriders. People who enjoy a good argument can go to Speakers' Corner (near Marble Arch tube station), where they can listen to people giving their views on a variety of topics to anyone who will listen.

Regent's Park, which was also originally a

WORD SEARCH

Can you find five words connected with royalty in the square? They are not all in the text. Some have been written vertically, some horizontally and some diagonally. (You will find the answers on page 138.)

B	H	R	Y	I	F	S	M
Q	C	O	N	B	D	E	O
U	R	Y	G	M	C	P	N
G	O	A	T	A	S	R	T
M	W	L	L	K	A	I	H
C	N	A	S	I	R	N	G
J	P	N	O	N	E	C	L
K	W	A	P	G	T	E	P

hunting park, is now the home of London Zoo, and an open air theatre which delights summer audiences with performances of Shakespeare's plays.

Not all the parks are in the centre of London. Greenwich, where the Maritime Museum is, and Richmond, famous for its beautiful trees and wild deer, are both in the suburbs.

Speakers' Corner.

Kensington and Knightsbridge

If you live in this area, the rent on your flat is probably very high – it is an exclusive part of London where you can find many foreign embassies, large, glamorous hotels, and the department store that is the symbol of expensive and high-class living – Harrods.

People say you can buy anything in Harrods, including wild animals – they even have a zoo which will sell you lion cubs as well as more common pets such as dogs, cats or parrots. Harrods succeeded in supplying one customer with a baby elephant, although it had to be ordered specially!

Harrods is not the only attraction here; there is the Albert Hall, where there is a festival of popular classical music concerts every summer known as 'the Proms'. Sporting events such as tennis tournaments and boxing matches are also held there.

Museums

Three of London's most interesting museums – the Victoria and Albert, the Science Museum and the Natural History Museum – are also in this area. The last, as its name suggests, has exhibits of birds, animals and reptiles as well as life-size reconstructions of prehistoric animals. The Victoria and Albert was founded with the aim of improving design in British manufacturing, but over the years it has expanded to include things from almost every place and period, including costumes from the theatre, and paintings. Finally there is the Science Museum, which is always crowded and is certainly the noisiest museum in London. It covers every aspect of science and technology, and the collections are constantly being moved round to make room for new acquisitions. They have inventions that did not become popular, such as the steam bicycle of 1912, and technological landmarks like the Cody biplane – the first aircraft to fly in England in 1912. In many of the rooms there are machines and computers that visitors can work themselves.

The audience at a 'Prom' concert.

WRITE

This is a **1** _____ plan of part of the Science **2** _____. If you come up the escalator, you will see the **3** _____ on the right. Next to them are the **4** _____. If you come up in the **5** _____, however, the first things you will see are the computers. The **6** _____ is near them. At the other end of the room, near the **7** _____ are some old **8** _____, and in the centre are the **9** _____. If you need the **10** _____, they are opposite!

What are the missing words? The answers are below.

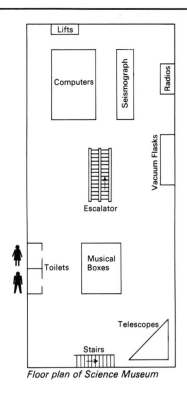

Floor plan of Science Museum

1 floor
2 museum
3 vacuum flasks
4 radios
5 lifts
6 seismograph
7 stairs
8 telescopes
9 musical boxes
10 toilets

Glossary

acquisition an item they have bought
ain't haven't (*slang*)
aristocracy the 'ruling class', sometimes connected with royalty
arrest to take prisoner
Barnet fair a festival in Barnet, an area of East London
barrister a lawyer who argues cases in a high court
behead to cut off someone's head
bowler hat a roundish black hat with a short brim
carol singers people who sing religious songs at Christmas, often to collect money for charity
charge (*n*) cost, expense, money
Civil Service government administration
civil war a war between two parts of the same country
coach a four-wheeled carriage with seats inside, pulled by horses
commemorate to honour the memory
commute to travel regularly a long distance between home and work
congested crowded
the Crown the King or Queen
daisy a small white and yellow flower
defendant an accused person
gent humorous word for 'gentleman'
goods things for sale
green (*n*) grass and trees
haberdashery a shop or department which sells small articles of clothing and sewing materials
house (*v*) to contain
in session working (a session is the time taken by one meeting of Parliament)
influential having influence; powerful

insurance a company which promises to pay a sum of money in case of illness or death, in return for regular payments

judicial legal

jury twelve people who decide in court if a defendant is innocent or guilty

legal representation help given to a defendant, usually by a barrister in court

Lord Mayor the leader of the group of people elected to govern London

marchers people in a procession, particularly on a protest march

metropolis the chief city of a country

nuclear weapons bombs which release atomic energy

nuffink nothing (*slang*)

old masters great painters of the 16th to 19th centuries

pillowcase a cover for a pillow (a cushion for your head on a bed)

pin-striped suit a suit made from material with very thin stripes

plague a deadly disease carried by rats

poppy a bright red flower

the press newspapers and magazines in general

Prime Minister the chief minister of a government

reptile a cold-blooded animal

residence a grand house where a public figure lives

restore to repair

sale when things are reduced in price in the shops

share (*n*) part ownership in a company

ship (*v*) to send by ship

slang very informal language (unsuitable for many situations)

solicitor a lawyer who gives advice and prepares legal documents

souvenir a thing bought or kept as a reminder of a place

stone by stone (to move) every stone of a building so that it can be exactly rebuilt in another place

store a shop

suburb an area on the edge of a city

tax money paid by citizens to the government for public purposes

traffic jam a queue of cars, lorries, buses, etc.

trial examination in a law court

warehouse a large building for storing things

wharf a place for tying up boats and ships

whodunnit a detective story (who's done it?)

wide range a large selection

wreath flowers woven in a circle

writing pad paper for writing letters

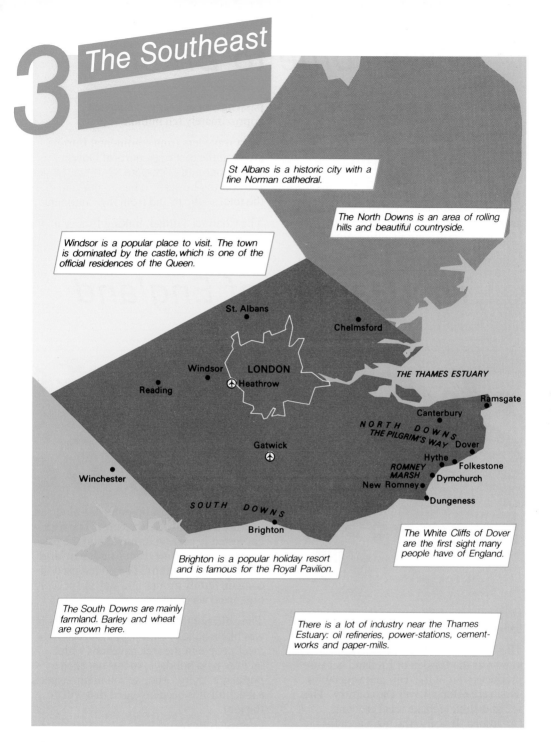

St Albans is a historic city with a fine Norman cathedral.

The North Downs is an area of rolling hills and beautiful countryside.

Windsor is a popular place to visit. The town is dominated by the castle, which is one of the official residences of the Queen.

St. Albans

Chelmsford

Windsor   LONDON

Reading   Heathrow

THE THAMES ESTUARY

Ramsgate

Canterbury

NORTH DOWNS
THE PILGRIM'S WAY   Dover

Gatwick

Hythe
ROMNEY
MARSH   Folkestone
New Romney   Dymchurch

Winchester

Dungeness

SOUTH DOWNS

Brighton

The White Cliffs of Dover are the first sight many people have of England.

Brighton is a popular holiday resort and is famous for the Royal Pavilion.

The South Downs are mainly farmland. Barley and wheat are grown here.

There is a lot of industry near the Thames Estuary: oil refineries, power-stations, cement-works and paper-mills.

The Southeast is the most densely-populated region of England. It is only 11 per cent of the land area of the country, but a third of the total population lives here. Because of this, a large part of the region is affected by urban development: housing, factories, offices and a complex network of roads and motorways. However, there is still attractive countryside to be found in all counties outside the influence of London. The south coast has a mild and sunny climate which makes it popular with both holiday-makers and the elderly, who find it a comfortable area to retire to.

Welcome to Britain

When you travel to Britain by sea or air, it is very likely that you will arrive in the Southeast, for this is where the main passenger ports and airports are located. Heathrow Airport, the world's busiest airport for international traffic, is about 20 miles (33 km.) east of central London, while Gatwick, the second major airport, is about thirty miles (50 km.) to the south. Heathrow has around twenty-eight million passengers per year and Gatwick approximately ten million.

Most travellers from continental Europe arrive at the east coast ports of Dover, Folkestone and Ramsgate. Of these, Dover is by far the busiest – it has 50 per cent of the total traffic to and from the Continent.

The Channel Tunnel, linking France to Britain, starts here.

The Garden of England

Do you know the names of these varieties of fruit?

They all grow in Kent, the county which is known as the Garden of England because it produces a lot of the fruit and vegetables which are eaten all over the country. The soil and climate make ideal growing conditions. It is also the main area for growing another kind of fruit called hops. You cannot eat them because they are very bitter, but they are an important flavouring for Britain's most popular alcoholic drink – beer! It is said that they also have medicinal properties, and local people sometimes put them in their pillows to sleep on as a cure for headaches!

The hop plants grow up poles and along an overhead framework like vines. The fruit is harvested in early autumn, and in the past people used to come from London in large numbers to pick hops. They often used to come in family groups and stay in specially organized accommodation.

They did not think it was hard work, for it was like a holiday with pay. Nowadays, most people in the area have jobs which include paid holidays, so it is not such a popular activity. And, as you might expect, a machine has been invented that will do the job!

Near the hop gardens are the oast-houses in which the hops are dried. They are of a very unusual design and are a very familiar sight in Kent.

These days, farmers have found that it is more economical to dry the hops in factories. Many of the oast-houses have been converted into fashionable houses.

Oast-houses.

GAME

As you have just been reading about the Garden of England, perhaps you would like to play this 'shopping' game. The first player begins by saying 'I went to the market and I bought' (for example) 'some apples'. The second player repeats this, and adds another item, for example, 'I went to the market and I bought some apples and some potatoes.' The third player has to repeat this sentence and add another item, and so it continues round the group until no one can remember any more!

TALKING POINT

Kent is known as the Garden of England. Which area of your country do you think could be called its garden?

Oh, I do like to be beside the seaside!

In Britain, you are never very far from the coast and there are lots of seaside towns, called resorts, all round the country where people go for their holiday or just on a day-trip.

Brighton, on the south coast, is a famous seaside resort. There are entertainments of all kinds. Brighton Pier is a popular place to spend a few hours, especially if the weather is not good enough to stay on the beach.

Brighton is also well known as a conference centre, and the major political parties, as well as the TUC, may hold their conferences there in the autumn.

DID YOU KNOW?

The major political parties in Britain are:

the Conservative Party (the Tory Party)
the Labour Party
the Liberal Party
the Social Democratic Party (the SDP)
the Social, Democratic and Liberal Party (also called the Social and Liberal Democrats)

TUC stands for 'Trades Union Congress'. This is an association of nearly all the unions.

The CBI is the equivalent association for employers. It stands for 'Confederation of British Industry'.

QUIZ

What do the following initials stand for? (You will find the answers on page 138.)

You will find the answers on page 138.

1 BBC **2 BR** **3 BA**
4 MP **5 UN** **6 EEC**

LOOK AND SAY

Talk about what you can see in the pictures below with a partner. Say what you like or don't like doing and find out what your partner enjoys. Also, say why you like or don't like these things.

Can you think of some more activities to talk about?

A Big Dipper

Windsurfing

Swimming

Fishing

Disco Dancing

Candy Floss

Space Invaders

Fish 'n' Chips

PRACTISE AND WRITE

Christopher has written a letter to his overseas penfriend, Ralf, telling him all about a typical British seaside holiday.

Write Ralf's letter in reply to Christopher saying what a seaside holiday is like in your country.

Use Christopher's letter as a model of how to start and finish your letter, and use contractions (eg *it's* not *it is*), because this is a letter to a friend you know well.

Seaview Boarding House,
Beach Avenue,
Brighton,
Sussex.

10th August

Dear Ralf,

On holiday at last! This is what I've been looking forward to for weeks. I wonder if a holiday at the seaside is the same in your country as in Britain? I'll tell you what it's like in Brighton anyway.

Everyone goes to the beach, of course, and even when the weather's not very warm you can see the families there wrapped up in sweaters sheltering next to their windbreaks! Some children like making sandcastles, while others enjoy paddling or playing ball. Sometimes there are donkeys on the sands for the children to ride on, but best of all is the Punch and Judy show. This is a puppet show. Punch – a wicked man who keeps hitting people (even his baby!) – and his wife, Judy. It's very funny!

Off the beach, I like the amusement arcades where you can play games like space invaders, and there are funfairs and rides like the big dipper or the big wheel. You can usually find all these things along the front or on the pier.

There are also certain kinds of food that people eat at the seaside. Of course, no seaside holiday would be complete without fish 'n' chips! They sell a lot of icecream as you can imagine, as well as candy floss (made from sugar and water) and rock. Rock is a hard sweet usually shaped like a stick, but the clever thing is that there's writing on it which goes all the way through. I don't know how they do it.

Anyway, to end this letter here is a seaside joke –

Question: "What do sea monsters eat?" Answer: "Fish and ships!".

Best Wishes,
Christopher

Are you a railway buff?

'Buff' is another word for enthusiast or fan. A railway buff is a person who is very interested in trains and railways and who knows a lot about them. Anyone who is a railway buff would be keen to visit the Romney, Hythe and Dymchurch Railway.

If you look closely at the photograph, it is clear why the railway is unusual. Its engines and carriages are one third the normal size. But this is not a toy railway. Hundreds of school children from Dymchurch use the train to go to school at New Romney throughout the year.

It was opened in 1927, and runs for 13.5 miles (22.5 km.) across Romney Marsh from Hythe to Dungeness – it is the longest miniature railway in the world. There are eleven steam locomotives and one diesel, over sixty coaches, fully equipped stations, and the trains pass at speed on the double track so that passengers get a good impression of what steam travel was like. It is privately owned, but there is a supporters' organization whose members (they are all railway buffs!) provide financial support and voluntary labour.

TALK AND WRITE

What is your favourite form of transport, and why do you prefer it?

Do you have a hobby? Write a paragraph about it saying what you do and why you find it interesting.

A tale of Canterbury

Canterbury is a town in Kent with a population of about 120,000. It is the religious capital of England because its cathedral is the seat of the Archbishop of Canterbury who is head of the Church of England.

From the 12th to the 15th centuries, it was a place of pilgrimage. Thousands of people came to pray at the shrine of a former Archbishop of Canterbury who was murdered in the Cathedral in 1170. His name was Thomas Becket.

Murder in the Cathedral

During the 12th century, King Henry II decided that the Church had too much power. In 1162, he made Thomas Becket Archbishop of Canterbury, thinking that his friend would help him to weaken the position of the Church. Although the King himself liked Thomas, he was not popular with other powerful men in England. They were jealous of his friendship with the King, and they also disliked him because he was not a nobleman. As Thomas was not even a priest, many people were very angry that he had been made Archbishop.

The King was amazed when Thomas began to defend the position of the Church against the King. After a while, Thomas had to leave England because relations between him and the King had become very bad, and Thomas was afraid that he might be killed. He lived in exile for five years until the King asked him to come back. The people, the bishops and the Pope were causing the King problems because they all wanted Thomas to continue as Archbishop of Canterbury.

When Thomas returned, in 1170, he brought authorization from the Pope to excommunicate the priests and noblemen who had acted against him. The King was furious when he learned this – soon afterwards, four of Henry's knights entered Canterbury Cathedral and murdered the Archbishop on the steps of the altar.

Three years later in 1173, Becket was made a saint, and his tomb became the

destination of thousands of pilgrims for three centuries. It was said that miracles happened there, and many sick people went there in the hope of finding a cure.

In the 16th century, when King Henry VIII separated from the Roman Catholic Church and established the Church of England, he said that Becket was no longer a saint, and his tomb was destroyed.

The story of Thomas Becket is the subject of two modern plays, *Murder in the Cathedral* by T.S. Eliot and *Becket* by Jean Anouilh.

WORDS

Find a word or words in the text which are similar in meaning to the following:

a hundred years   liked by a lot of people
envious   very surprised   return   very angry

Chaucer's pilgrims

The best-known Canterbury pilgrims are probably those who appear in the book by Geoffrey Chaucer, *The Canterbury Tales*. It was written in the 14th century, when the pilgrimage had become a rather pleasant holiday for the groups of people who travelled together for protection and companionship.

The Canterbury Tales is a collection of stories told by the members of a group of pilgrims. Through the stories we get a vivid picture not only of the narrators themselves but also of the religious and social life of the 14th century. There were twenty-nine pilgrims altogether, including a knight, a doctor, a miller, a middle-aged widow and numerous members of religious orders of one kind or another.

The Pilgrim's Way is the name of an old path starting at Winchester which, it is traditionally thought, was taken by pilgrims travelling to Canterbury. However, there is no real evidence of this. You can still walk along some of the route, which is part of a long-distance footpath called the North Downs Way. It is protected by law, so it cannot be ploughed by farmers or made into a motorway!

If you have the energy to follow the route as far as Canterbury, you will find that although there is no tomb, Becket is not forgotten. His face and name are still there, on postcards and souvenirs in every other shop!

A twentieth-century visitor
The most famous modern 'pilgrim' is without doubt Pope John Paul II. His visit to Canterbury in 1982 was an important historical event because it showed the spirit of understanding that exists now between the Roman Catholic and the Anglican Churches.

The Archbishop of Canterbury, Archbishop Runcie, and the Pope knelt in silence on Becket's steps – just 817 years after his murder.

Pilgrims on their way to Canterbury.

ASK AND ANSWER

Use the correct form of the verb in brackets.

1 Where . . . . . Becket . . . . . *(murder)*?
2 When . . . . . Becket . . . . . *(die)*?
3 Why . . . . . *(be)* noblemen jealous of Becket?
4 How long . . . . . *(stay)* . . . . . in exile?
5 Who . . . . . *(write)* 'Murder in the Cathedral'?
6 What . . . . . Chaucer . . . . . *(write)*?
7 Why . . . . . the footpath . . . . . *(protect)*?
8 Why . . . . . the Pope . . . . . *(visit)* Canterbury?

WHAT DO THEY DO?

Chaucer's pilgrims had different jobs. Do you know what we call people who do *these* jobs?

a "My mother tries to cure people who are ill."
   She's a . . . .
b "His brother drives lorries all over the country."
   He's a . . . .
c "My great-grandfather used to make flour."
   He was a . . . .
d "I want to look after people's teeth when I grow up."
   I want to be a . . . .
e "John repairs cars for a living."
   He's a . . . .
f "Do you know anyone who designs houses?"
   Do you know any . . . ?

The stockbroker belt

The Stockbroker Belt is the popular name for the county of Surrey, which has become a residential area (or 'belt') for London commuters. Although the word 'stockbroker' refers to a particular occupation – it is someone who works at the Stock Exchange – many different professional groups live here. The roads are lined with trees and there are large detached houses with well-kept gardens. Most people associate this area with the rich life-style of those people who work in the City of London.

Commuters are not only found in Surrey of course! People travel daily to work in London from all over the Southeast: from Brighton on the south coast, from Chelmsford in the north-east of the region, from Reading in the west, and from everywhere in between!

People who can live close to their place of work usually hate the idea of spending so much of their lives travelling. No doubt many commuters feel the same way, but there are some for whom it has become quite an enjoyable way of life. Train commuters pass the time in a variety of ways. There is the crossword, the newspaper, a good book, or office work, but some people have found more unusual activities. One set of travellers wanted to make the most of the two hours they spent travelling each day and so they organized themselves into groups, each with a 'teacher', to study French, car maintenance and other subjects of interest. One train even had a club called the 6.18 club (it was called this because their train left the station at 6.18 each morning). It had about thirty members who all played golf together after work. They had their own newsletter and a club tie, and the committee meetings were held on the train!

From time to time, proposals are put forward to try and improve the situation at the 'rush-hour' when over a million and a quarter commuters arrive and leave Central London at the same time each day. Until now, none of these has been acceptable to either employers or employees. So people who are not commuters still have to make sure that they travel at quieter times in order to avoid being crushed to death by the workforce of London!

FIND QUESTIONS FOR THESE ANSWERS

1 They work at the London Stock Exchange.
2 From all over the Southeast of England.
3 Because they don't want to spend a lot of time travelling.
4 They do office work.
5 Because the train left the station at that time.
6 Over a million and a quarter.
7 To avoid the crowds.

Glossary

authorization permission to do something

big dipper small carriages on a big curved track that take you up and down through water at the fair

big wheel a huge wheel which you can sit in as it rotates high into the air

boarding house a private house where you pay to stay and have breakfast and perhaps an evening meal

carriage the place for passengers on a train

cement grey powder mixed with water and used for building

club tie a necktie with a special design worn by members of a group or club

conference a meeting to exchange ideas and opinions

continental Europe the mainland of Europe

contraction abbreviation

convert (v) to change

county an administrative area of the UK

crush (v) to press till something breaks

destination the place to which someone or something is going

detached a house which is not attached to any others

diesel engine a train which uses oil as fuel

excommunicate to expel from the Church

framework the part of a structure that gives support

front a road beside the sea where people can walk

funfair an amusement park

knight a nobleman, usually military

lined with things in lines

live in exile having to live away from one's own country, usually as a punishment

living (n) way of earning money

locomotive engine

maintenance keeping in good working condition

medicinal properties capable of curing illness

miniature very small but exactly like the normal sized object

miracle an act which cannot be explained by the laws of nature

monster a huge and frightening animal

'n' abbreviation of 'and'

narrator a person telling a story

nobleman a man in a position of power through his birth

in large numbers many people together

paddle (v) to walk in water just a few inches deep

pier a metal construction stretching out to sea

pilgrimage a journey to a holy place

power station a building where electric power is generated

priest a minister of the Christian Church

properties qualities, characteristics

refinery place where oil is purified (refined)

religious order group of people living under religious rules

residential area the part of the town where people live

retire to give up work, usually around the age of 60

rush-hour times when crowds of people travel to and from work

sandcastle a small castle made at the beach out of sand, usually by children

seat the place, or base, from which the Archbishop works

shrine a tomb containing holy remains eg bones or clothing

space invaders a computerized game

sweater a woollen piece of clothing with long sleeves

tomb the place where a dead person is buried, usually large and decorated

track a steel line on which trains run

urban of the town or city

vine a plant which produces grapes

voluntary not paid to do a job

windbreak something made of cloth which is used to give protection from the wind

windsurf to surf on a board with a sail

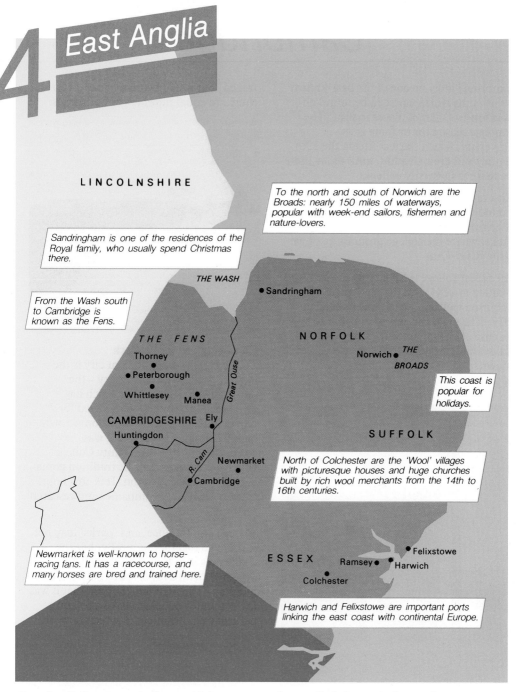

4 East Anglia

LINCOLNSHIRE

To the north and south of Norwich are the Broads: nearly 150 miles of waterways, popular with week-end sailors, fishermen and nature-lovers.

Sandringham is one of the residences of the Royal family, who usually spend Christmas there.

THE WASH

• Sandringham

From the Wash south to Cambridge is known as the Fens.

THE FENS

Thorney
•
• Peterborough
•
Whittlesey   Manea

NORFOLK

Norwich • *THE BROADS*

This coast is popular for holidays.

Great Ouse

CAMBRIDGESHIRE Ely
Huntingdon

SUFFOLK

R. Cam
Newmarket
•
• Cambridge

North of Colchester are the 'Wool' villages with picturesque houses and huge churches built by rich wool merchants from the 14th to 16th centuries.

Newmarket is well-known to horse-racing fans. It has a racecourse, and many horses are bred and trained here.

ESSEX   Ramsey •   • Felixstowe
• Harwich

Colchester •

Harwich and Felixstowe are important ports linking the east coast with continental Europe.

East Anglia is extremely flat, and it is dominated by agriculture. It has beautiful cities with fine historic buildings (such as Cambridge, Ely, Norwich, Peterborough and Colchester), and it has many sandy beaches and inland waterways.

In medieval times, it became rich because of the wool trade. It was not affected by the industrial revolution, and even today there is very little heavy industry. It was, however, the home of the agricultural revolution and is now best known as a farming region.

It is rather isolated from the rest of Britain because of its position away from the main national routes and because of its shape. It is more than half surrounded by sea.

41

Cambridge

Cambridge must be one of the best-known towns in the world, and can be found on most tourists' lists of places to visit. The principal reason for its fame is its University, which started during the 13th century and grew steadily, until today there are more than twenty colleges.

Most of them allow visitors to enter the grounds and courtyards. The most popular place from which to view them is from the Backs, where the college grounds go down to the River Cam.

The oldest college is Peterhouse, which was founded in 1284, and the most recent is Robinson College, which was opened in 1977. The most famous is probably King's, because of its magnificent chapel. Its choir of boys and undergraduates is also very well known.

King's College Chapel.

The University was exclusively for men until 1871 when the first women's college was opened. Another was opened two years later and a third in 1954. In the 1970s, most colleges opened their doors to both men and women. Almost all the colleges are now

mixed, but it will be many years before there are equal numbers of both sexes.

Cambridge Science Park

To the North of this ancient city is the modern face of the University – the Cambridge Science Park, which has developed in response to the need for universities to increase their contact with high technology industry. It was established in 1970 by Trinity College, which has a long scientific tradition going back to Sir Isaac Newton. It is now home to more than sixty companies and research institutes.

The ideas of 'science' and 'parks' may not seem to go together naturally, but the whole area is in fact very attractively designed, with a lot of space between each building. The planners thought that it was important for people to have a pleasant, park-like environment in which to work.

TALKING POINTS

- What is the purpose of a science park?
- What are the advantages to the University and to industry?

WRITE

Every year, thousands of students come to Cambridge from overseas to study English. Here is a letter from Frieda, a German student, to an Italian friend. Write a reply to Frieda's letter, telling her what has happened to you recently.

High Trees,
Hills Road,
Cambridge.

July 3rd

Dear Anna,

I have been studying English in Cambridge for two months now, and I have had a wonderful time.

Perhaps the most exciting thing that has happened to me was going to a May Ball. Let me explain — every year in June (although they're called May Balls!) the colleges organize big dances with lovely food and champagne served from marquees in the college grounds. The dance goes on all night, and then, at dawn, people take a boat and have breakfast on the river. For a May ball the students wear dinner jackets and bow ties, and long dresses, although they usually wear jeans and tee-shirts!

Before the ball, I met the friends I was going with in a typical Cambridge student pub called 'The Bath'. Apparantly there's an old student joke : "If my mother rings, tell her I'm in 'The Bath'."

One Saturday I went down to the river to watch the 'bumps', which is a rowing competition between colleges. Each boat tries to overtake or 'bump' another boat. Lots of people got very wet!

I have found that you can learn a lot just by being in England! Yesterday, I learnt a new expression — Hobson's choice. Apparently a man called Thomas Hobson lived in cambridge about 200 years ago. He had about forty horses, and whenever a customer wanted to hire one, he always gave them the one that had rested longest. The only choice was 'Hobson's choice', that is no choice at all, and that's what it means today!

Please write soon and tell me what you've been doing recently.

Lots of love,
Frieda.

The Fen Country

The area known as the Fens covers part of three different counties: Lincolnshire, Cambridgeshire and Norfolk. The main part is about 40 miles (67 km) northwards from Cambridge to the Wash and about 40 miles south-eastwards from Peterborough.

A fen is land which is low-lying and wet, often partly covered with water. The Fen Country consists of miles of flat land with almost no trees or hedges. It is divided by high banks that contain the rivers and drains, which help to control the level of water in the fields. The small fenland towns and villages used to be islands in the time before the area was drained, and many of their names show this – eg Whittles*ey*, Rams*ey*, Thorn*ey*, Man*ea*. Both *-ey* and *-ea* mean 'island'.

Fenland characters

Work on the drainage of the Fens was started by a Dutchman, Cornelius Vermuyden, in the 1630s, but they were not completely drained until the late 19th century. Because of this, the Fenland villages were isolated from the rest of the country for many centuries, and 'Fenmen' were regarded with a lot of suspicion. Some people thought they had webbed feet! This, of course, was not true, but they *did* use

stilts to move across flooded areas. They have a reputation for being fighters (they are known even today as 'Fen Tigers') which is partly because a well-known English rebel, Oliver Cromwell, came from the Fens.

Oliver Cromwell was brought up in Huntingdon, on the edge of the Fens, and found plenty of support there when he formed an army against the King at the start of the Civil War.

The Fens today

Now that the drainage of the Fens is complete, the area has some of the richest and most expensive farmland in the country. The black, fertile soil produces sugar-beet, potatoes, and celery, as well as cereals.

A lot of fruit is grown in this area too. During the summer, when the fruit is picked, students come from different countries in Europe to work on the farms. In this way, they can earn some money, have a holiday and improve their English all at the same time!

The area is, of course, much richer than it was in the days when men made their living from fishing and catching wildfowl, although mechanized farming has caused some social problems: there are fewer jobs, and the population is smaller because young people have moved to the larger towns and cities to look for work.

However, it is not short of visitors, particularly those who are interested in wildfowl (watching it, more than shooting it these days!).

An area known as the Ouse Washes is allowed to flood naturally and provides a perfect area for thousands of ducks, geese and swans which spend the winter there. The swans are of two types, Bewick and

Whooper, and they fly from eastern Russia each year. Sometimes there are as many as 2,000 swans which arrive in family parties, having survived the dangerous journey. At night, part of the Wash where many of the swans come to be fed is floodlit, and the sight and sound of so many beautiful birds is magical.

TRUE OR FALSE?

1 Before the Fens were drained, people in the Fens used to make their living from farming.
2 Work began on draining the Fens in the first half of the 17th century.
3 People were suspicious of Fenmen because they did not know very much about them.
4 The swans can be found on the Ouse Washes all the year round.
5 Part of the Wash is floodlit so that the swans can be fed.
6 Modern farming methods have made the area prosperous.

WORD SEARCH

In the square below, ten words are hidden. They are all connected with the Fens. How many can you find?

S	H	A	D	P	S	T	K	L	G	Y	B
T	O	B	L	T	I	G	E	R	P	I	O
I	D	I	N	R	S	P	A	B	I	S	R
N	K	U	L	F	W	H	T	D	M	L	Q
C	Y	O	T	D	A	N	E	R	J	A	N
A	F	E	N	V	N	L	Q	A	D	N	C
F	W	H	Z	O	P	C	J	I	U	D	V
L	G	R	I	K	M	E	T	N	F	S	W
A	J	E	N	S	D	L	F	L	O	O	D
T	O	A	F	Q	B	E	G	B	Z	K	O
A	B	T	G	L	F	R	I	P	E	F	E
H	E	Y	H	M	A	Y	A	Y	M	R	H

(You will find the answers on page 138.)

Let's go shopping in Norwich

Norwich is the most important city of East Anglia and of course it has a large shopping centre for the rural area surrounding it. It also has to cater for the tourists who are attracted to the city by such features as the cathedral, museums and castle.

Unlike many cities, where small specialist shops have gradually been replaced by large department stores and supermarkets, Norwich still has a wide variety of shops.

One of the most unusual must be the Mustard Shop. As its name suggests, it sells nothing but mustard, and there are as many different kinds as it is possible to imagine. It has a mustard museum, which describes the history of Colman's mustard. The Colmans were a famous Norwich family who started a mustard-making business over 150 years ago.

Then there is the outdoor market, with its multi-coloured stall-covers, where you can buy everything from books to bananas.

Britain's oldest recorded town

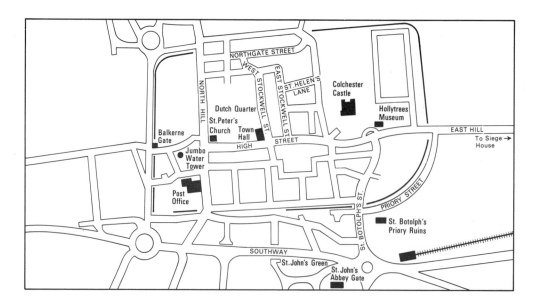

If you go for a walk through the streets of Colchester, you will be able to see evidence of its long history (and indeed the history of England) almost everywhere you look. This town trail will take you past the most famous buildings and give you some information about their importance in the development of the town. As you read, follow the route on the map. There are pictures to show you the locations of the buildings which are described.

Colchester town trail

1 The trail starts at Balkerne Gate, which used to be the West Gate of the town in Roman times, and is one of the best-preserved Roman gateways in Britain. The Romans invaded Britain in AD 43, and Colchester became a town for retired Roman soldiers. The road beyond the gateway is a modern by-pass, but beside it you can see the original Roman walls.

2 Walk towards the town centre along Balkerne Passage and you cannot miss 'Jumbo', the town's most famous landmark. It is a Victorian water-tower which took its name from a famous elephant sold to a circus in 1882, the year of the tower's construction.

3 Go up the hill into the High Street, one of the main streets during Roman times, past the Town Hall, and turn left into West Stockwell Street. Walk down to Northgate Street and back up East Stockwell Street and you will see some fine mediaeval and Georgian houses, most of which have been restored. This area is known as the Dutch Quarter because it is where Flemish weavers lived when they fled from the Netherlands in the 16th century. They helped to improve the Colchester cloth industry.

4 Turn left along St Helen's Lane. Near St Helen's Chapel, on the corner, are the remains of one of the walls of a Roman Theatre.

5 Next on the itinerary are the Castle and Museum, so our route takes us back to the High Street and left a short way, to the gates of Castle Park. The Castle, which dates from the 11th century, was built on the site of a Roman temple. Now

Balkerne Gate.

The Dutch Quarter.

there is a museum inside, where you will find a wonderful collection of Roman antiquities and a lot of information about Roman Colchester.

6 Leaving the Castle, turn left down East Hill to look at the Siege House. During the Civil War, Colchester was defended by a Royalist Army and was besieged for eleven weeks before finally surrendering. Bullet-holes made during the siege can still be seen clearly in the walls.

Of course there are many other interesting places to visit in this historic town, but no doubt by now you will be ready to return to the Town Centre in search of tea and cakes!

Do you like oysters?
Colchester has been famous for its oysters from the River Colne since the time of the Romans. The season starts in October, and every year the Mayor of Colchester goes out in a boat with a party of guests to fish the first oysters. In the evening, the Oyster Feast is held in the Town Hall. Well-known people, usually television personalities, are invited as well as local people.

Colchester Castle.

WARNING!
It is said that oysters should only be eaten when there is an 'r' in the month. When should you **not** eat oysters?

DO YOU KNOW?

1 If you were shopping in a British town, where would you go to buy:
apples a joint of beef carrots
a jar of jam a newspaper books?

2 What could you buy in these shops:
an ironmonger's a delicatessen
a tobacconist's?

LOOK AND WRITE

The cloth industry **used to** be more important in Colchester. Of course, in an old town like this, a lot of things have changed. For example, buildings that **used to** be there have been replaced by others, or they no longer exist.

Write sentences about Colchester with **used to**.
Here are some ideas:
Flemish weavers/The Dutch Quarter
Roman Theatre/St Helen's Chapel
Colchester Castle/Roman Temple
Balkerne Gate/West Gate

Glossary

agriculture farming

antiquities works of art remaining from old times

ball a formal dance

besiege to attack

bow tie a tie made in the shape of a bow, usually worn with a dinner jacket

bullet something fired from a gun

by-pass a road which goes round the edge of a town, avoiding the town centre

cater for to provide facilities (shops, hotels, etc) for

celery a kind of vegetable

cereal grains such as corn, wheat, oats and barley

continental Europe Europe except the British Isles

dawn (*n*) sunrise

delicatessen a shop that sells 'special', usually non-British, food

dinner-jacket a man's black jacket worn on formal occasions

dominated by agriculture mainly farmland

drain (*v*) to reduce or get rid of water

expression a phrase

fan (*n*) an admirer, supporter

fertile rich soil where things grow easily

flood (*v*) to cover with water

floodlit lit with very strong lights

grounds large gardens of a house

hedge a line of bushes, often forming a boundary between fields

inland waterway a system of rivers and lakes joined together and not connected with the sea

itinerary a route

ironmonger a person who sells things made of metal

joint a particular cut of meat

landmark usually a building that is easily seen from a distance

location a position in the town

marquee a very large tent

mechanized farming farming which makes use of machines

oyster a kind of shellfish

preserved in good condition

prosperous rich, wealthy

quarter an area (of a town)

rebel (*n*) a person who rejects authority, eg a government

recorded town a town described in old books

remains the parts of an old building which are left after it has fallen down or disappeared

reputation what people say

restored repaired and modernized

retired too old to work

rural of the country

season the time when the oysters are ready to eat

siege an attack

stilts long wooden poles with support for the feet, designed so that you can walk without your feet touching the ground

sugar-beet a plant from which sugar is made

tent a construction made of canvas, used for sleeping in when camping

trail a path, a route that can be followed

TV personalities people who are famous because they appear on TV

water tower a reservoir or tank for the distribution of water in an area

weaver a person who makes cloth

webbed feet feet with the toes joined, eg ducks have webbed feet

wildfowl wild ducks or geese

Liverpool is one of Britain's major ports and has long had an important ship-building industry.

Manchester and Sheffield are large industrial centres. Sheffield is famous for steel.

Manchester

Liverpool

Sheffield

The moorland and hills of Staffordshire and Derbyshire are part of the Peak District.

Shropshire is the birthplace of the industrial revolution. Ironbridge, where iron was first made, is a living museum.

PEAK DISTRICT

DERBYSHIRE

STAFFORDSHIRE

SHROPSHIRE

Leicester

THE MIDLANDS

Ironbridge

R. Severn

Birmingham

Coventry is famous for its magnificent modern cathedral. The waters of Leamington Spa can cure medical problems.

Coventry R. Avon

THE BLACK COUNTRY

Leamington Spa

Warwick

MALVERN HILLS

Worcester

Stratford-upon-Avon

Hereford

South of Birmingham lies the historic town of Warwick with its great castle. Nearby is Stratford-upon-Avon, the birthplace of William Shakespeare.

In the beautiful fruit-growing countryside of the Severn valley, are the famous cathedral-towns of Worcester, Hereford and Gloucester, plus ancient Tewkesbury.

Tewkesbury

Gloucester

COTSWOLD HILLS

R. Thames

Oxford

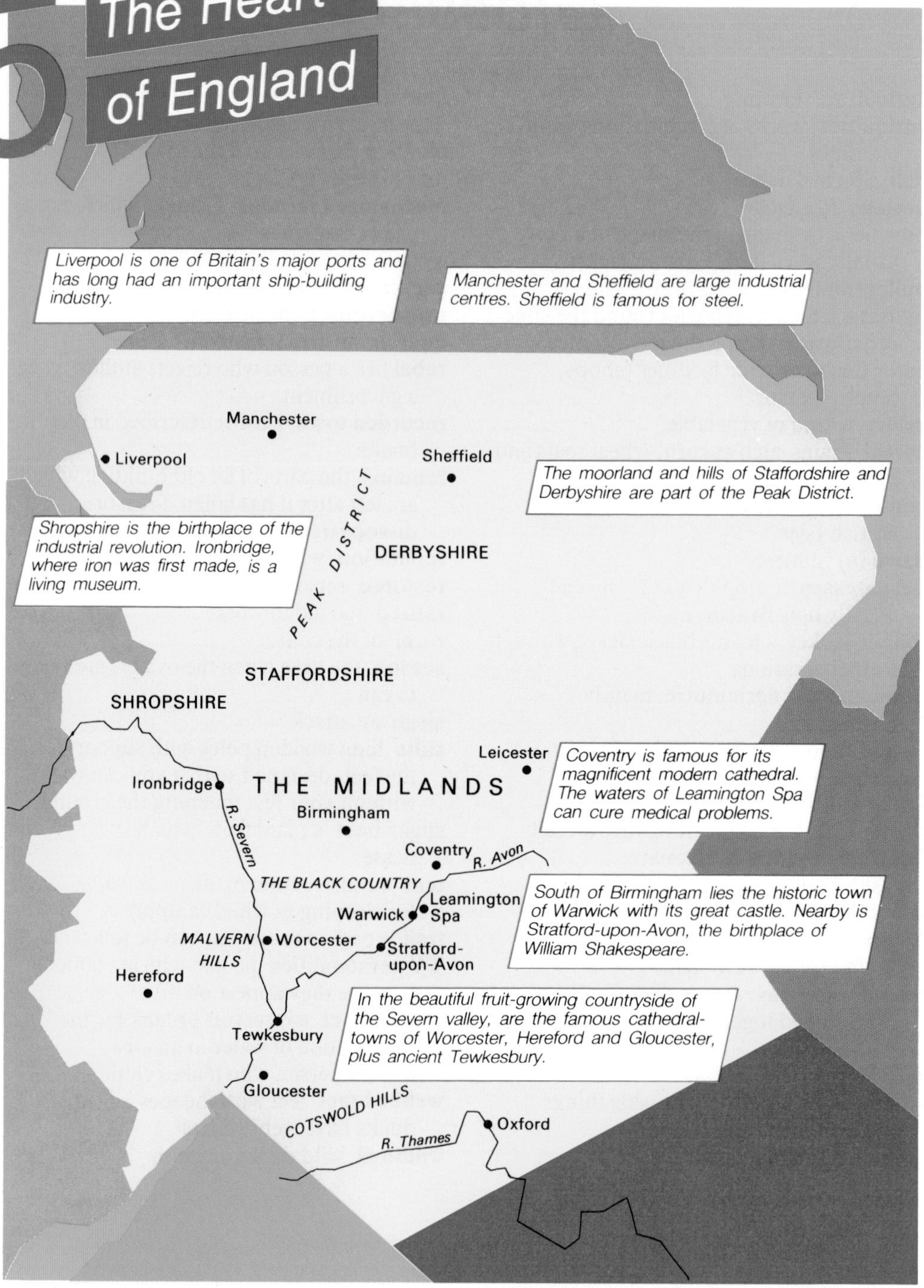

Birmingham is the most important city in the Midlands, one of England's most productive regions, with large industrial areas such as the Black Country in the West Midlands. However, there is also a lot of farming country, for example in the counties of Shropshire, Worcestershire and Leicestershire. This region has some beautiful countryside in the Peak District National Park, the Cotswold Hills and the Malvern Hills.

The Swan of Avon

In April 1564 a son was born to John and Mary Shakespeare at Henley Street, Stratford-upon-Avon. His mother was the daughter of Robert Arden, an important farmer in Warwickshire. His father was a rich citizen whose business was making and selling leather gloves.

The parents did not guess that their son, William, was going to be such an important figure in English poetry and drama, and that his plays would still be acted four hundred years later – not only in England, but all over the world!

While still a teenager of nineteen, William married Anne Hathaway, a farmer's daughter some years older than himself.

Anne Hathaway's cottage.

We don't know how he earned his living during these early years. He may have helped his father in the family business or he may have been a country schoolmaster for a time. During these years his three children were born: Susannah, the eldest, then twins – a son, Hamnet (not Hamlet!), and another girl, Judith. In 1587 Shakespeare went to work in London, leaving Anne and the children at home. One story says this is because he killed some deer which belonged to a rich landowner nearby, and that he had to run away from the law.

Shakespeare soon began to act and to write plays. By 1592 he was an important member of a well-known acting company, and in 1599 the famous Globe Theatre was built on the south bank of the river Thames. It was in this theatre that most of his plays were performed and, like all Elizabethan theatres, it was a round building with the stage in the centre open to the sky. If it rained, the actors got wet! If the weather was too bad, there was no performance.

By 1603, the year when Queen Elizabeth I died, Shakespeare was already the leading poet and dramatist of his time. He continued to write for the next ten years, but in 1613 he finally stopped writing and went to live in Stratford where he died in 1616. He is buried in Holy Trinity Church, Stratford-upon-Avon.

Ben Jonson, who lived from 1572 to 1637, and who was also a famous writer of plays, called Shakespeare 'Sweet swan of Avon'. Shakespeare has been known as the 'Swan of Avon' ever since.

LOOK AND PRACTISE

Can you say these dates?

1600 sixteen hundred
1608 sixteen oh eight
1610 sixteen ten
1621 sixteen twenty-one
1632 sixteen thirty-two

ASK

Ask questions to get these answers.
1 1564.
2 For four hundred years.
3 In 1583.
4 Susannah.
5 In the Globe Theatre.
6 In 1603.
7 In Holy Trinity Church.
8 Because it lies beside the River Avon.

BIRTH

Where was | he | born?
          | she |

Shakespeare | was born in | Stratford.
Elizabeth I | | Greenwich.

MARRIAGE

When did he get married?
Shakespeare got married at nineteen.

Who did he marry?
He married Anne Hathaway.

When did she get married?
Elizabeth I never got married.

DEATH

When did he die?
Shakespeare died in 1616.

When did she die?
Elizabeth I died in 1603.

Now talk about these people in the same way with a partner.

Elizabeth I was born in Greenwich Palace in London in 1533. She was the daughter of Henry VIII and Anne Boleyn. She became Queen of England on the death of her sister, Mary, in 1558 and was a very popular and strong queen. During her reign England became very important in European politics, in commerce and the arts. She died in 1603.

Name	Birth	Marriage	Death
Queen Victoria	London, 1819	Albert of Saxe-Coburg	1901
Sir Winston Churchill	Blenheim Palace, 1874	Clementine Hozier	1965
Jane Austen	Steventon, Hampshire, 1775	–	1817
John Lennon	Liverpool, 1940	Yoko Ono	1980
Henry VIII	Greenwich Palace, 1491	1 Catherine of Aragon 2 Anne Boleyn 3 Jane Seymour 4 Anne of Cleves 5 Catherine Howard 6 Catherine Parr	1547

Birmingham
– the market place

Buying and selling has been an important part of life in Birmingham for more than eight hundred years. In fact men used to sell their wives there as recently as the 18th century! (In 1733 Samuel Whitehouse sold his wife to Thomas Griffiths in the market place for a little more than one pound!) Although neither husbands nor wives are for sale nowadays, Birmingham's markets offer a large choice of *other* goods.

Each Tuesday, Friday and Saturday, the colourful rag market can be found. People used to come to buy and sell old clothes (rags) but now there is a wide selection of modern fashions for everybody.

Years ago farmers used to sell their animals at the Bull Ring, but now it is one of the biggest open-air markets and shopping centres in the United Kingdom. People enjoy shopping there because it has modern shops, together with the atmosphere of a traditional street market.

TALKING POINT

Describe any famous markets you have visited and the kinds of things you have bought.

A cathedral of our time

Coventry Cathedral. The great entrance porch links the new cathedral to the ruins of the old cathedral. On the wall is Epstein's famous statue of St Michael in triumph over the devil.

In 1962 a magnificent new cathedral was consecrated in Coventry, and bishops and archbishops from all over the world attended. They came to see a cathedral of our time, built using the skills and ideas of our day.

During the Second World War, the old cathedral had been destroyed in a terrible night of bombs which killed many people in the city. Only the walls of the cathedral remained but people immediately made a new altar with the fallen stones. The altar cross was made from burnt wood and nails from the ruins. Immediately after the war, a similar nail cross was taken to Kiel in Germany as a sign of friendship, and a stone from the ruins of Kiel Cathedral was given to Coventry in return. This is the Kiel Stone of Forgiveness, now in the Chapel of Unity.

Also after the war a group of young Germans helped to clear one corner of the ruined cathedral.

Today this area is the Centre for International Understanding where young people of all nationalities can meet.

The new cathedral looks very modern, but it is joined physically and spiritually with the old. Together they remind us of the madness of war.

TALKING POINTS

- Why do you think the ruins of the old cathedral were left standing?
- The title calls this a cathedral of our time. Why? Can you think of more than one reason?
- The author of this text writes of 'the madness of war'. Do you agree? Is war ever justified?

Oxford

Town and gown

There has been a town where Oxford now stands for many centuries – even before 912, the first written record of its existence.

The University began to establish itself in the middle of the 12th century, and by 1300 there were already 1,500 students. At this time, Oxford was a wealthy town, but by the middle of the 14th century, it was poorer, because of a decline in trade and because of the terrible plague, which killed many people in England. Relations between the students and the townspeople were very unfriendly, and there was often fighting in the streets. On 10th February 1355, the festival of St Scholastica, a battle began which lasted two days. Sixty-two students were killed. The townspeople were punished for this in two ways: they had to walk through the town to attend a special service on every St Scholastica's day until 1825. Worse than this, the University was given control of the town for nearly 600 years.

Nowadays, there are about 12,000 students in Oxford, and the University and the town live happily side by side!

The Rover Group factory in Cowley.

City of dreaming spires

The best-known description of Oxford is by Matthew Arnold, the 19th century poet, who wrote about 'that sweet city with her dreaming spires'.

However, Oxford is not only famous for its architecture. In the 20th century, it has developed quickly as an industrial and commercial centre. The Rover Group factory at Cowley, for example, is an important part of Britain's motor industry.

Some of the famous Oxford colleges.

It is also an important centre in the world of medicine; it is the home of Oxfam, the charity which raises millions of pounds to help poor people all over the world; and its airport contains Europe's leading air-training school.

Oxford words

The Oxford English Dictionary is well-known to students of English everywhere. The new edition, published in 1989, defines more than half a million words, and there are twenty volumes.

Some of the words are special Oxford words. For example, 'bulldog' in Oxford is the name given to University policemen who wear bowler hats and sometimes patrol the streets at night. They are very fast runners. 'Punt' is a word often used in both Oxford and Cambridge. It refers to a flat-bottomed boat with sloping ends which is moved by pushing a long pole in the water.

An English bulldog.

An Oxford 'bulldog'.

Oxford University Press, the publishing house which produces the Oxford English Dictionary, has a special department called the Oxford Word and Language Service (OWLS for short). If you have a question about the meaning of a word or its origin, you can write or telephone, and the staff there will help you.

TRUE OR FALSE?

1 There was no town at Oxford before 912.
2 Oxford has always been a wealthy town.
3 The people of Oxford were punished for the trouble with the students.
4 The University used to be more important than the town.
5 Oxford is famous for its architecture.
6 Britain's motor industry is based in Cowley.
7 The word 'bulldog' usually means 'policeman'.
8 Oxford is a city of contrasts.

Punting–a favourite Oxford pastime.

LOOK AND PRACTISE

EXCUSE ME, COULD YOU TELL US HOW TO GET TO THE CATHEDRAL?

YES...ER...GO RIGHT, LEFT, AND THEN LEFT, NO RIGHT, AGAIN, AND ...ER...NO-GO LEFT THEN... THEN ASK AGAIN....

Asking the way is easy. Understanding the answer is much more difficult! Here are some replies. Can you say what the question was? One of you should read the replies while your partner looks at the map.

1 You are standing outside Christ Church College.
'Turn right towards Carfax. Continue in the same direction until you get to the Randolph Hotel. Then turn left and it is immediately on your right.'

2 You are in Broad Street outside the Sheldonian Theatre.
'Turn right and walk to the crossroads. Keep straight on into Holywell Street and continue down Longwall Street to the High Street. Turn right and then first left into Merton Street. Follow this and you will find it on your left.'

3 You are in front of the Town Hall.
'Turn right at Carfax, and walk all the way down High Street. You'll see it just before the bridge, opposite Magdalen College. It's about a ten-minute walk.'

4 You are on Magdalen Bridge.
'Follow High Street in the direction of Carfax. Turn right into Turl Street, and then left into Market Street. Then it'll be on your left.'

Now describe how to get to these places: the hotel from the Cathedral, the Town Hall from the Sheldonian, the Botanic Garden from Jesus College, the deer park from Blue Boar Street. Try and practise the expressions you have just used.

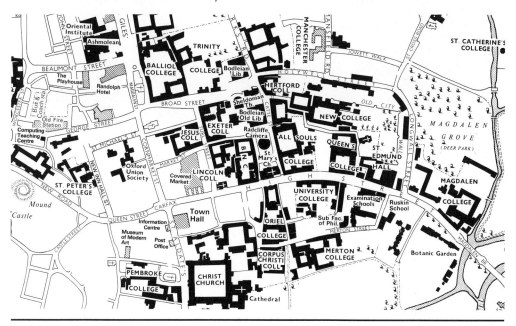

TALKING POINT

Britain has over 2,000 miles of canals, and some of the most interesting can be found in this area of England. In recent years, canal boat holidays have become more and more popular because they offer an opportunity to see the countryside away from the noise of busy roads.

Here is an advertisement for a canal cruiser holiday. Discuss what you will need for such a holiday and who you would like to go with!

CASTLINE CRUISERS
Over 80 Boats Operating from 4 Bases

The Canal Wharf, Binbury, Nr. Torpley, Cheshire CA3 8TS, England. Tel. (0349) 542879

You can enjoy beautiful corners of the English countryside, and get away from the crowds.

On our cruiser holidays, you are free to go wherever you want and stop wherever you want.

Navigating the canals is one of the most exciting parts of the holiday! We give you full instruction on navigation, and you'll find it no problem at all.

Your cruiser will have all the comforts of home: cooker, fridge, shower, hot and cold water, and most have central heating.

These are just some of the canals you can travel along. Hire your cruiser from one of these centres.

Liverpool and the Beatles

On Wednesday 24th October 1962, *Love Me Do*, entered the British Top Thirty. It was the first single by an unknown group from Liverpool called the Beatles. It was the first of a number of big hits that would make John Lennon, Paul McCartney, George Harrison and Ringo Starr the most successful pop group the world has ever known.

The early years
However, the road to success was not always easy. John and Paul had spent many afternoons listening to American stars like Chuck Berry and Elvis Presley before they were able to write the famous Lennon and McCartney songs.

Although the long evenings spent playing in hot nightclubs in Liverpool and Hamburg in Germany had not earned them much money, they found the experience very useful when playing to huge audiences later on.

Not only was their style of singing new and exciting but their unusual haircuts – Beatle 'mops'! – and crazy sense of humour immediately became the latest fashion.

Influences
One of the most important people at the start of their careers was Brian Epstein, a Liverpudlian record-dealer. He managed to change four ordinary working-class lads into international superstars. George Martin, their record producer, encouraged them to introduce all kinds of unusual instruments on their records and combined popular and classical styles in a new and original way.

The 1960s
During the 1960s the Beatles were always in the news headlines; films, world tours and sometimes scandal. John once suggested that the Beatles were better known than Jesus Christ. This caused hundreds of young Americans to burn their Beatle records. In addition some people thought there were hidden messages about drugs in some of the songs.

ASK AND ANSWER
Look at the hit parade then ask and answer questions like the following examples.

- What was number one? *Telstar*
- Which record moved up two places? *Venus in Blue Jeans* by Mark Wynter.
- Which record came in at number 27? *Love Me Do* by the Beatles.

Bring this week's Top Thirty to class and ask similar questions.

NME TOP THIRTY

(Wednesday, October 24, 1962)

Last Week	This Week			
1	1	TELSTAR Tornados (Decca)
2	2	THE LOCO-MOTION Little Eva (London)
4	3	SHEILA Tommy Roe (HMV)
5	4	RAMBLIN' ROSE Nat Cole (Capitol)
3	5	RAIN UNTIL SEPTEMBER Carole King (London)
8	6	VENUS IN BLUE JEANS Mark Wynter (Pye)
11	7	LET'S DANCE Chris Montez (London)
–	8	LOVESICK BLUES Frank Ifield (Columbia)
6	9	YOU DON'T KNOW ME Ray Charles (HMV)
10	10	WHAT NOW MY LOVE Shirley Bassey (Columbia)
16	11	SWISS MAID Del Shannon (London)
12	12	SHERRY Four Seasons (Stateside)
7	13	SHE'S NOT YOU Elvis Presley (RCA)
19	14	DEVIL WOMAN Marty Robbins (CBS)
9	15	IT'LL BE ME Cliff Richard (Columbia)
–	16	SHE TAUGHT ME HOW TO YODEL Frank Ifield (Columbia)
13	17	I REMEMBER YOU Frank Ifield (Columbia)
15	18	LONELY Acker Bilk (Columbia)
–	19	NO ONE CAN MAKE MY SUNSHINE SMILE Everly Bros. (Warner Bros.)
14	20	DON'T THAT BEAT ALL Adam Faith (Parlophone)
17	21	IT STARTED ALL OVER AGAIN Brenda Lee (Brunswick)
23	22	SEND ME THE PILLOW YOU DREAM ON Johnny Tillotson (London)
25	23	THE PAY-OFF Kenny Ball (Pye)
21	24	IF A MAN ANSWERS Bobby Darin (Capitol)
28	25	BOBBY'S GIRL Susan Maughan (Philips)
–	26	BECAUSE OF LOVE Billy Fury (Decca)
–	27	LOVE ME DO Beatles (Parlophone)
26	28	REMINISCING Buddy Holly (Coral)
18	29	ROSES ARE RED Ronnie Carroll (Philips)
–	30	THE JAMES BOND THEME John Barry (Columbia)

Break-up

After a decade of successful music and films, the Beatles finally decided to break up in the early seventies, after public disagreements about money and personalities.

Although many fans hoped there would be a reunion throughout the 1970s, this became impossible with the tragic murder of John Lennon in New York in 1980.

The surviving Beatles are still deeply involved in musical and film projects, but many fans still long for the music of the 60s.

LOOK AND PRACTISE

Someone from Liverpool is called a *Liverpudlian*. If you come from the United States you are called an *American*. What do you call the people who come from these towns and countries?
1 England 2 Scotland 3 Ireland
4 Dublin 5 Greece 6 Spain
7 Holland 8 France 9 London
10 The USSR.
(You will find the answers on page 138.)

ASK AND ANSWER

A friend of yours is writing an article about the history of pop music for a new rock magazine. He/she wants some information on the Beatles. See if you can help him/her.

"What was their first hit?"
"Tell me, is it true they used to play a lot in Hamburg?"
"How did their early experience help them later on in their careers?"
"But people thought their hair styles were terrible, didn't they?"
"What was George Martin's role actually?"
"Why did some Americans burn their records?"
"Why did they break up in the end?"
"Do you think they'll ever get together again?"

Glossary

altar a special table at the front of a church

architecture art of designing buildings

bowler hats a roundish black hat with a short brim

break up to separate

charity an organisation which helps people, without making a profit

county an administrative area of the UK

cruiser a small pleasure boat with an engine which has room for sleeping.

decade ten years

decline (*n*) a decrease

dramatist writer of plays

fans enthusiastic supporters

forgiveness willingness to pardon, not to want to punish someone

get together to join, unite

headlines the most important pieces of news in the newspaper or on TV or radio

hidden messages secret information

hit a successful record

lad a young man

leading most important

long (*adv*) for a long time

madness insanity

navigating steering a boat in the right direction

patrol (*v*) to go round the streets to make sure that everything is all right

plague a deadly disease carried by rats

pole a long rounded piece of wood or metal

run away from the law to run away from the police

single a record with one song on each side

skills knowledge and experience; abilities

staff a group of assistants who work under a manager

superstars extremely famous people in entertainment

top thirty the 30 most popular songs based on the sales of records in the shops

wealthy very rich

wharf a place to tie up boats and ships

working class belonging to the class of people who work in manual labour eg in factories

6 The Dales to the Border

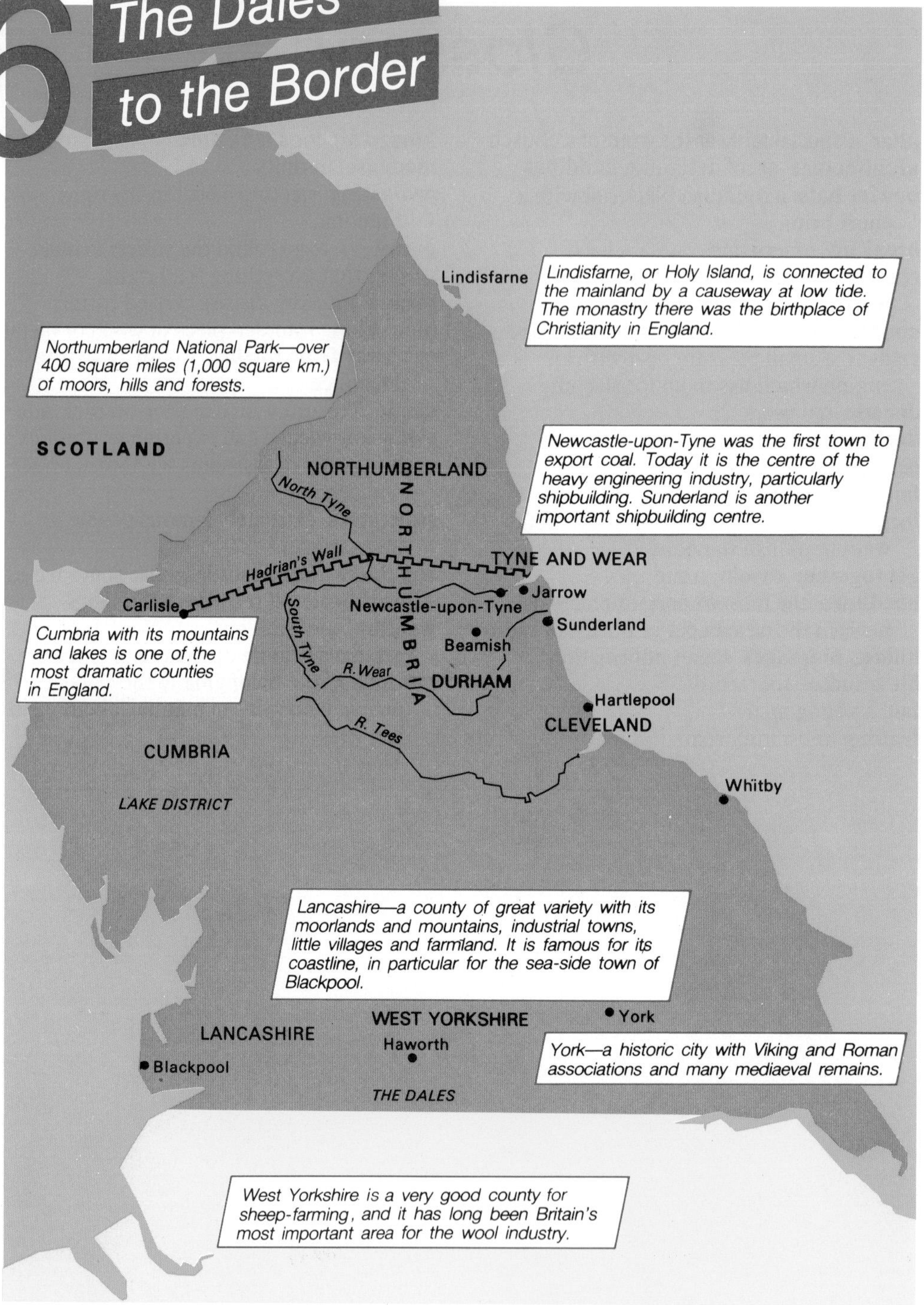

Lindisfarne

Lindisfarne, or Holy Island, is connected to the mainland by a causeway at low tide. The monastry there was the birthplace of Christianity in England.

Northumberland National Park—over 400 square miles (1,000 square km.) of moors, hills and forests.

SCOTLAND

NORTHUMBERLAND

North Tyne

Newcastle-upon-Tyne was the first town to export coal. Today it is the centre of the heavy engineering industry, particularly shipbuilding. Sunderland is another important shipbuilding centre.

Hadrian's Wall

TYNE AND WEAR

Carlisle

Jarrow

NORTHUMBRIA

Newcastle-upon-Tyne

Sunderland

Cumbria with its mountains and lakes is one of the most dramatic counties in England.

South Tyne

Beamish

R. Wear

DURHAM

Hartlepool

R. Tees

CLEVELAND

CUMBRIA

Whitby

LAKE DISTRICT

Lancashire—a county of great variety with its moorlands and mountains, industrial towns, little villages and farmland. It is famous for its coastline, in particular for the sea-side town of Blackpool.

LANCASHIRE

WEST YORKSHIRE

Haworth

York

York—a historic city with Viking and Roman associations and many mediaeval remains.

Blackpool

THE DALES

West Yorkshire is a very good county for sheep-farming, and it has long been Britain's most important area for the wool industry.

This northernmost region of England contains some of the wildest and loneliest parts in the country, but also some of the busiest industrial centres. The Ice Age formed many deep valleys in the counties of Cumbria and North Yorkshire, made rivers into waterfalls and left behind hills and mountains. Beneath the earth is coal – the foundation of the region's industry.

Northumbria

5,000 years of industry

There are four counties in the region of Northumbria. They are Tyne and Wear, Cleveland, Durham and Northumberland. This is a region of great natural beauty although industry of some kind has existed here for thousands of years.

Industry and the sea

There has been a fishing industry in Northumbria probably since the middle of the 13th century. Wooden ships were built for fishing and for trading and this industry grew and grew, particularly during the 18th century. By 1850 the building of iron steamships became a major industry on the rivers Tyne, Wear and Tees. One hundred years ago a quarter of the world's ships were built in Northumbria. Today, sadly, this industry is disappearing.

Above is a picture of H.M.S. Warrior, the world's first iron battleship. It is over 130 years old. Now it lies in Portsmouth harbour, where it is open to visitors.

The Industrial Revolution

About 200 years ago a period of great industrial growth began in Britain. This growth was fed by coal and steam power.

During the 19th century the Northeast of England led the world in many types of heavy industry. You have already read about iron steamships. In addition, there were railway engineering, bridge building, industrial machinery, and for the making of all this – iron and steel production.

There was also an important textile industry. Both Yorkshire with its wool and Lancashire with its cotton were major textile-producing areas at this time.

You can learn a lot about this period by visiting an industrial museum like the one at Beamish.

TALKING POINTS

- Would you like to visit a museum like this? Why?
- What would interest you most?
- Are museums generally boring?
- How can they be made interesting?

Beamish
North of England
Open Air Museum

There's something here to interest the whole family! Take a short journey on a steam train from an old station, have a ride on a 1920's Gateshead electric tramcar, go down an old mine to see how coal was mined, warm yourself at a coal fire in one of the pit-men's cottages and smell the home baked bread, see the animals and old farm tools at Home Farm – a picture of North Eastern life more than half a century ago.

Pleasant Tea Room and souvenir shop.

Open April till September every day 10–6. October till March, every day, except Monday, 10–5. (Last admission 1 hour before closing time). Enquiries: Telephone Stanley (0207) 31811.

LOOK AND PRACTISE

There is	a major	shipbuilding	industry	in . . .
	an important	fishing		near . . .
		textile		
		engineering		

Coal is mined in . . .
Oil is refined near . . .

Iron and steel are produced in . . .
Chemicals are made near . . .

Cars are manufactured in . . .

Work with a partner and take it in turns to make similar sentences using the map and the key opposite. Then write down all the sentences you have made.

LOOK IT UP

1 Use the map on page 62 to label the major rivers on this map.
2 Write in the names of the four counties.
3 Work with a partner. Ask and answer questions on your maps beginning with: Where . . . ? What's the name of . . . ?

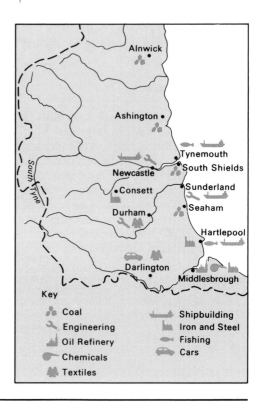

Key

- 🐝 Coal
- ✎ Engineering
- ⛽ Oil Refinery
- 🛢 Chemicals
- 🏭 Textiles
- ⛴ Shipbuilding
- 🏭 Iron and Steel
- 🐟 Fishing
- 🚗 Cars

Industrial misery

During the Industrial Revolution, many people moved from the country to the towns, where they usually lived in dirty and overcrowded conditions. They worked long hours for very little money. Even small children had to work in the factories and mines. Many writers, in particular Charles Dickens, have written about their misery. He wrote this description of one of the new industrial towns:

> 'It was a town of red brick, or of brick that would have been red if the smoke and ashes had allowed it. It was a town of machinery and tall chimneys out of which smoke came for ever and ever. It had a black canal in it and a river that ran purple with bad-smelling dye.'

Today the noise and smoke of factories from the time of Dickens have been replaced by modern industry, and the 19th century slums have been cleared. But this region – like many others – has been badly affected by the post-industrial recession. Unemployment is very high, as it was in the 1930s when economic depression forced men and women on to the dole queues, and things became so bad that a hunger march was organized from Jarrow to London. The 1980s have also seen dole queues and unemployment marches from the North towards London. Many of the traditional heavy industries are disappearing, and the region is developing new technological industries to help it overcome its difficulties. These include electrical engineering, plastics, fine chemicals, computers, and North Sea oil and gas.

- Is unemployment a problem in *your* country?
- Do you know anyone who is unemployed?
- What can be done to solve the problem?

The most beautiful corner of England

The Lake District is the central mountainous area of Cumbria in the Northwest and has some of England's most beautiful scenery. Several other names are used to describe this area, for example Lakeland, and the English Lakes. Since the Lake District is a National Park, there is special control over building, to make sure that the beauty of the countryside is not spoiled. Nearly one quarter of the Lake District National Park is owned by the National Trust.

The National Trust is a charity, which means it is financed by ordinary people who pay to become members. It is *not* financed or run by the government.

The Trust was set up in 1895 by three people who thought that industrialization could spoil the countryside and ancient buildings of England and Wales.

Today the Trust is the third largest landowner in the country. It owns about 586,000 acres (almost 2,400 sq. km.) of land. Its properties include famous gardens, whole villages, farms, wind- and water-mills, lakes and hills, abbeys, prehistoric and Roman antiquities (including part of Hadrian's Wall), important bird sanctuaries such as Lindisfarne Island in Northumberland, and examples of industrial archaeology.

The aim of the Trust is to conserve all these things for our enjoyment.

TALKING POINTS

- Is there an organization in your country that is similar to the National Trust?
- How important is it to conserve areas and buildings?
- Can conservation stop progress?

Ghosts of Yorkshire

The Brontës of Haworth

In one of the loneliest parts of the wild Yorkshire moors lies the village of Haworth.

People say the parsonage at Haworth is haunted by the ghosts of the brilliant, tragic Brontës. Along ancient streets, the ghosts of the three sisters, Charlotte, Emily and Anne walk among the crowds. Branwell, their brother, still sits silently in the corner of the old pub.

Imagination perhaps, but this is a place of dreams. Lost in a world of windswept loneliness, the Brontës wrote those 19th century stories that we still love to read: *Jane Eyre, Wuthering Heights, The Tenant of Wildfell Hall*, are as dramatic today as ever. And for miles around the moors, the grim, grey stones remind us of their novels, which take place in this wild countryside.

But fame came to them late, and this talented family all died young: Branwell, a ruined man; solitary Emily; gentle Anne within months of her success. Charlotte was the only one of the family to get married. Tragically, she died before giving birth to her first child.

In spite of the sadness of their lives, the Brontës have passed on their experience of beauty and passion. In their novels, you can breathe the atmosphere of the moors and feel the powerful personalities of these famous novelists.

The parsonage at Haworth is haunted . . .

COMPLETE

Emily, Charlotte and Anne are the names of three ... and Branwell was their brother. Their ... was Brontë. They lived in a ... in Haworth some time between the year ... and the year 1900, and they are famous for the ... which they .... *Jane Eyre, Wuthering Heights* and *The Tenant of Wildfell Hall* are ... of their .... Their own story is sad because they were all ... when they died and only one of them was ever ....
(You will find the answers on page 139.)

LOOK AND READ

1 The author writes about the 'tragic' Brontës. What words and phrases can you find which give the idea of sadness and tragedy? Example: 'loneliness'.
2 Notice the poetic effect of combining the real, physical world with the world of inner feelings as in 'a place of dreams'. Can you find another example?
3 Repetition of certain sounds can create an atmosphere. Notice the repetition of 'l' and 'w' in 'lost in a world of windswept loneliness'. Can you find another example of alliteration (sound repetition)?

Dracula!

The Yorkshire seaside town of Whitby is a busy little fishing port which has changed little for the past 300 years. The town is famous for its associations with Captain Cook – the famous 18th century explorer – and for one other thing . . .

From the old streets around the harbour 199 steps lead up to the church of St Mary. It was the churchyard to St Mary's which gave the writer, Bram Stoker, the idea for his world-famous book *Dracula*.

For a long time people have believed that creatures called vampires lived in Central Europe. Vampires are dead people who come back at night to drink the blood of living people!

Dracula, written in 1897, is the story of a vampire from Transylvania who travelled to England. When his ship was damaged in a terrible storm, Dracula – the vampire – jumped to land at Whitby in the shape of a huge dog!

Then, the churchyard became a place of horror!

The oldest ghost?

The city of York was an important centre for the Romans, who built a camp where York Minster stands today. During recent excavations under the Minster a man who was working there saw half a Roman soldier marching towards him. As the soldier came nearer he saw the other half below the level of the floor. Then he understood that the man was walking at the level of the old Roman Road. The soldier walked past and slowly disappeared.

Most ghosts seem to die after about four centuries, but the ghost of the Roman soldier in York is nearly nineteen hundred years old!

TALKING POINTS

- Do you know any ghost stories about the area where you live? If so, tell them to the class.
- Would you spend the night alone in a haunted house? What would you take with you?
- Do you believe in ghosts? Why/why not? What about vampires?

The historic city of York

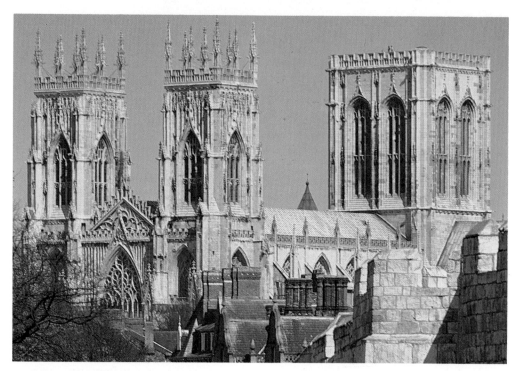

Yorvik was the capital of a Viking kingdom. In mediaeval times, York was the second city of the land. Georgian York was the social centre of the North, Victorian York was an important railway centre, and 20th century York is, among other things, the home of world-famous chocolate and one of the most beautiful cities in the world.

Think of York and then think of historic things: battlements, glorious churches, ancient narrow streets, old houses and welcoming pubs where stories of ghosts are told around the fire. Then visit York and find these impressions true, even the ghost stories!

As well as being an example of living history, the city knows well how to show its history to visitors. The National Railway Museum's collection of steam trains and Royal Carriages is world-famous. In the Castle Museum one can imagine oneself in a 19th century world of Victorian streets, shops, farmhouses and homes. York Story, in Castlegate, is a lively museum showing how the city of York grew during 1900

years. In the newest museum visitors travel in a special electric car (like a time machine) through an original Viking street with the sights, sounds and smells which a Viking in York would have experienced.

Most splendid of all, of course, is the magnificent Minster. It is the largest Gothic cathedral in northern Europe and the most important church in the North of England. It is famous for its mediaeval stained glass windows, and the interior is full of colour and light. You can see the huge Minster for miles. You can climb to the top of the tower, go on a guided tour or take a trip into history below ground, where you can see the Roman remains.

Feeling energetic? Nothing could be better than a walk along the top of the three-mile city walls.

In today's York there is a festival of music and the arts every summer, which includes the famous miracle plays. These are the religious plays which were performed in the streets in mediaeval York and which are still enjoyed in York today.

PUZZLE

Many streets in York end in the word 'gate', like Castlegate. 'Gate' was the Viking word for 'street'. How many words can you make from the letters in CASTLEGATE?

How many words can you find in this word?

CASTLEGATE

least ___ ___ ___
cat ___ ___ ___
___ ___ ___

Glossary

associations connections
battlements a wall around a castle or town, with holes to shoot through
causeway a raised road across water
churchyard a burial ground round a church
conserve (*v*) to keep and protect
dole money given by the government to unemployed people. 'To be on the dole' or 'to join the dole queue' means to be unemployed
dye (*n*) a chemical used to colour things
excavation digging to find old, historical things
grim severe, unfriendly
haunt (*v*) to live in a house as a ghost
hunger march (*n*) a walk organized by people who are protesting against unemployment and hunger
mainland the main part of a country or continent, without islands
mediaeval of the period of history between 1100 and 1500, the Middle Ages
monastery a place where monks live as a community

moor a wild, open, often high area
overcrowded with too many people
parsonage a house where a parson (priest) lives
recession decline of business and trade
refine to make pure
ruined (*adj*) destroyed by failure, caused for example by drinking too much
run (*v*) to organize, administer
sanctuary an area where birds, animals or plants are protected from man and other enemies
slums area of poor, dirty houses or flats
stained glass coloured glass
talented (*adj*) with a natural ability to do something well
textile concerned with cloth
time machine a machine which takes you into the past or future
vampire a dead person who drinks the blood of living people
waterfall a river which falls over rocks or cliffs
windswept without shelter from cold winds

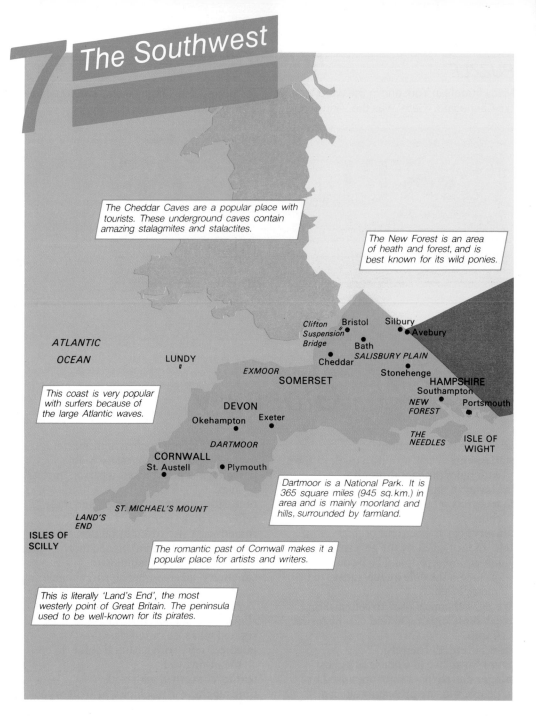

The Cheddar Caves are a popular place with tourists. These underground caves contain amazing stalagmites and stalactites.

The New Forest is an area of heath and forest, and is best known for its wild ponies.

ATLANTIC OCEAN

LUNDY

Clifton Suspension Bridge

Bristol

Silbury

Avebury

Bath

Cheddar

SALISBURY PLAIN

Stonehenge

EXMOOR

SOMERSET

HAMPSHIRE

Southampton

NEW FOREST

Portsmouth

This coast is very popular with surfers because of the large Atlantic waves.

DEVON

Okehampton

Exeter

THE NEEDLES

ISLE OF WIGHT

DARTMOOR

CORNWALL

St. Austell

Plymouth

Dartmoor is a National Park. It is 365 square miles (945 sq.km.) in area and is mainly moorland and hills, surrounded by farmland.

ST. MICHAEL'S MOUNT

LAND'S END

ISLES OF SCILLY

The romantic past of Cornwall makes it a popular place for artists and writers.

This is literally 'Land's End', the most westerly point of Great Britain. The peninsula used to be well-known for its pirates.

The principal industries here are farming and tourism. Although there are some very big farms, most are small family farms with a mixture of cows, sheep and cereal crops. The main emphasis is on dairy products – milk and butter. On Exmoor and Dartmoor, two areas of higher land, conditions are ideal for rearing sheep and beef-cattle.

Industry is centred on three large ports: Bristol in the north, and Portsmouth and Southampton in the south-east. In Bristol, aircraft are designed and built. In Portsmouth and Southampton, the main industries are shipbuilding and oil-refining.

Holiday time in the West Country

The counties of Devon, Cornwall and Somerset are often called the West Country. They have always been popular with holiday-makers, so there are a large number of hotels, caravan- and camping-sites and private houses and farms which offer bed and breakfast. People enjoy going there because of the beautiful countryside, where they can 'get away from it all', and because the coastline offers the best beaches and surfing in England. Also, the weather is usually warmer than in the rest of the country!

The completion of two motorways, the M4 from London and the M5 from Birmingham, has meant that people can travel to the West Country much more easily nowadays. However, the arrival of large numbers of people at certain times of the year (especially at bank holidays, when almost everyone has a day off) can lead to traffic jams on the motorways going in and out of the West Country. Then you may find the pretty Devon lanes blocked by cars pulling caravans!

West Country food

Do you enjoy eating local food? If you do, you will like the West Country.

Most people who visit Devon look forward to having a cream tea. This consists of a pot of tea (of course!) and scones served with strawberry jam and cream. The cream is not the same as that found in the rest of the country. It is called clotted cream, and it is much thicker and yellower than ordinary cream. What are scones? Well, here is a recipe which you can try yourselves. By the way, in Devon they are called 'chudleighs'.

If you are still hungry you could try a Cornish pasty!

Pasties used to be the main food of Cornish miners and fishermen about 150 years ago, because they provided a convenient meal to take to work. They were made of pastry which had either sweet or savoury fillings, and were marked with the owner's initials on one end. This was so that if he did not eat all his pasty at once he would know which one belonged to him!

Now a visit to Somerset, which has always been famous for its cheeses. The most popular variety is probably 'Cheddar', which is a firm cheese. It usually has a rather mild flavour but if it is left to ripen, it tastes stronger, and is sold in the shops as 'mature Cheddar'. It takes its name from a small town which is also a beauty-spot well-known for its caves, which contain stalagmites and stalactites.

Ingredients

8oz (250g) flour 1½ oz (25g) butter
3 level teaspoons ½ oz (15g) caster sugar
baking powder ¼ pt (140ml) milk
pinch of salt

Method

Sieve flour, baking powder and salt into a bowl. Rub in butter. Add sugar and mix to a soft dough with milk. Roll out to about ½ inch (1cm) thick, cut into rounds and place on baking sheet. Brush with milk. Bake near the top of a hot oven, 230°C, gas mark 8, for 12-15 minutes. Leave to cool and serve with jam and thick cream.

Finally, a West Country drink. No visit would be complete without a pint of Somerset cider, or 'Scrumpy' as it is called. Cider is made from apples and is sold all over the United Kingdom, but scrumpy is much stronger, and usually has small pieces of the fruit floating in it. Most people find that they have to be very careful about how much they drink!

WRITE

Write a recipe in the same way as the one for scones. If possible, choose a local speciality.

FOOD QUIZ

1 Why do you have to be careful about drinking 'scrumpy'?
2 What is 'mature' cheddar?
3 How is ordinary cream different from clotted cream?
4 Why were Cornish pasties popular with workmen?

Magic circles

Stonehenge.

The county of Wiltshire is most famous for the great stone monuments of Stonehenge and Avebury, and the huge earth pyramid of Silbury. No written records exist of the origins of these features and they have always been surrounded by mystery.

Stonehenge is the best known and probably the most remarkable of prehistoric remains in the UK. It has stood on Salisbury Plain for about 4,000 years. There have been many different theories about its original use and although modern methods of investigation have extended our knowledge, no one is certain why it was built.

One theory is that it was a place from where stars and planets could be observed. It was discovered that the positions of some of the stones related to the movements of the sun and moon, so that the stones could be used as a calendar to predict such things as eclipses.

At one time, people thought that Stonehenge was a Druid temple. The Druids were a Celtic religious group who were suppressed in Great Britain soon after the Roman Conquest. Some people believe that they were a group of priests, while others regard them as medicine-men who practised human sacrifice and cannibalism.

Because Stonehenge had existed 1,000 years before the arrival of the Druids, this theory has been rejected, but it is possible that the Druids used it as a temple. The theory is kept alive today by members of a group called the 'Most Ancient Order of Druids' who perform mystic rites at dawn on the summer solstice. Every year, they meet at Stonehenge to greet the first midsummer sunlight as it falls on the stones and they lay out symbolic elements of fire, water, bread, salt and a rose.

Another interesting theory is that the great stone circle was used to store terrestrial energy, which was then generated across the country, possibly through 'ley lines'. 'Ley lines' is the name given to invisible lines which link up ancient sites throughout Britain. They were thought to be tracks by which prehistoric man travelled about the country, but now many people believe that they are mysterious channels for a special kind of power. Ley lines are international. In Ireland, they are known as 'fairy roads', in China they are known as *lungmei* and are believed to extend all over the Earth, and in Australia, the Aborigines make ceremonial journeys for hundreds of miles along these secret tracks.

Alongside the theories of the scholars are local legends. Here is one.

> Stonehenge was built by the devil in a single night. He flew backwards and forwards between Ireland and Salisbury Plain carrying the stones one by one and setting them in place. As he worked, he laughed to himself. 'That will make people think. They'll never know how the stones came here!' But a friar was hiding in a ditch nearby. He surprised the devil, who threw a stone which hit the friar on the heel.

Is the story true? Well, the stone which the devil threw, known as the 'heel stone', can still be seen by the side of the road. However, geologists have shown that the stones came from South Wales and north Wiltshire, not Ireland!

WRITE

Write down the questions for these answers.

1 Because there are no written records.
2 About 4,000 years.
3 Because of the way the stones were arranged.
4 They were a Celtic religious group.
5 On the summer solstice.
6 Fire, water, bread, salt and a rose.
7 Fairy roads.
8 South Wales and north Wiltshire.

The text describes different theories and stories about the origins of Stonehenge, and about the people who used it. Look carefully at the text and make a list of all the theories. Here are some examples:

Perhaps Stonehenge was a Druid temple. It might have been used to store terrestial energy.
Some people believe that the Druids were a group of advanced thinkers.

Offshore islands

There are between 120 and 130 offshore islands which can be classified as part of England's natural geography. Some are privately owned, some are inhabited, while others are only known to lighthouse-keepers, sailors and naturalists. The attraction of these islands is different to different people. Ornithologists for example might want to study a rare seabird; archaeologists might be interested in a prehistoric or early Christian site; sociologists might study why certain islands have been deserted or resettled.

The Isle of Wight (1) is the largest island off the south coast. Charles I was once imprisoned here, and there is a large prison, Parkhurst, on the island today. A lot of its attractive scenery has formed as a result of a thick layer of chalk – the white teeth of the 'Needles' are the most famous example.

Many of the inhabitants travel daily to the mainland to work. Those who work on the island are usually involved with the tourist industry because the island is visited by thousands of tourists every year. A favourite activity is yachting.

The Isles of Scilly (2) can be found 28 miles (45 km.) southwest of Land's End. There are between 50 and 100 'islands' in the group (some are just large rocks) but only six are inhabited. In early spring, they export beautiful flowers to the mainland.

St Michael's Mount (3) is linked to the mainland at low tide by a causeway. It was a base for the tin trade at one time and, because of its religious connection with Mont-Saint-Michel in France, it was also a trading and migration centre from the earliest days of Christianity.

Finally, between the coast of Devon and South Wales is the island of *Lundy* (4), which is three miles long and half a mile wide. At one time it was almost a pirate kingdom, but today it is a bird sanctuary, with a resident human population of about twelve.

The sea – ships and sailors

Nelson's flagship, the 'Victory'.

The coastline of the Southwest of England stretches for 650 miles (over 1,000 km.), and has many different features: cliffs, sand, sheltered harbours, estuaries and marshes. It is not surprising that much of the activity in this region has been inspired by the sea.

Side by side on the south coast of Hampshire are the two ports of Portsmouth and Southampton. Portsmouth is the home of the Royal Navy, and its dockyard has a lot of interesting buildings and monuments. There is also the Royal Naval museum, where the main attraction is Horatio Nelson's flagship, the 'Victory'. Southampton, on the other hand, is a civilian port for continental ferries, big liners, and oil and general cargo.

Many great sailors had associations with the West Country, for example Sir Walter Raleigh, the Elizabethan explorer, and Horatio Nelson, who lived in Bath in Somerset. The most famous sailor of recent times, was Sir Francis Chichester, who returned to Plymouth after sailing round the world alone in 'Gypsy Moth'.

In Bristol, to the north, one of the largest Victorian steamships, the 'Great Britain', has been restored. It was the first iron ocean-going steamship in the world and was designed by a civil and mechanical engineer with the unusual name of Isambard Kingdom Brunel (1806–1859). He not only designed three ships (including the first transatlantic steamer, the 'Great Western'), but also several docks and a new type of railway that enabled trains to travel at greater speeds. He also designed the first ever tunnel underneath the Thames and the Clifton Suspension Bridge.

Unfortunately, this coastline, in particular that of Cornwall, is famous – or infamous – in another way too. The 'foot' of Cornwall has the worst of the winter gales, and in recorded history there have been more than fifteen shipwrecks for every mile of coastline. There is even a shipwreck centre and museum near St Austell where you can see an amazing collection of items that have been taken from wrecks over the years. There are a lot of stories about Cornish 'wreckers' who, it is said, tied lanterns to the tails of cows on cliff-tops or put them on lonely beaches when the weather was bad, so that ships would sail towards the lights and break up on the dangerous rocks near the coast. The wreckers would then be able to steal anything valuable that was washed up on to the shore.

GAME

'Shipwrecked'. Imagine that you have been shipwrecked. Seven people have survived but there is only room for four people in the lifeboat. Work in groups of seven. You must each think of reasons why *you* should have a place in the boat and the others be thrown into the sea! (*Or* each member chooses to be a famous person and must explain why they should survive.) Then tell the other members of the group. Finally you should all vote to decide who has the best reasons for surviving!

A famous shipwreck

A shipwreck that has received a lot of attention is the 'Mary Rose', which was built at Portsmouth over 400 years ago on the orders of Henry VIII. He was watching the ship sailing out with 60 others, when suddenly she sank for no apparent reason. Perhaps she was overloaded. Whatever the reason, she sank within minutes, and almost all of the 700 crew were drowned.

The ship lay undisturbed in soft mud until the 1970s, when marine archaeologists and a team of divers began exploring the wreck. They discovered that the hull was complete and that there was a huge variety of artefacts, for example clothes and shoes as well as pottery and metal and wooden objects.

The 'Mary Rose', and artefacts found in her wreck.

WORDS

Here is a list of people and things they study. Match the people in the left-hand column with the subjects in the right-hand column. Work with a partner and ask and answer like this:

WHAT DO ORNITHOLOGISTS STUDY?

BIRDS

sociologists	animal life
geologists	living things
archaeologists	people in groups
zoologists	rocks
botanists	ancient things
biologists	the stars
linguists	plant life
astronomers	languages
etymologists	animals and plants in their natural environment
naturalists	the origins of words

Use a dictionary to check your answers.

Glossary

artefact something made by human beings

baking powder a powder used instead of yeast to make cakes rise

Bank Holiday a public holiday

beauty-spot a place people visit because it is beautiful

cannibalism eating human flesh

castor sugar very fine sugar

chaos great confusion

cliff a steep rock

deserted empty, lonely

devil the spirit of evil, Satan

ditch a narrow channel dug in a field

dough a mixture of flour and water or milk

eclipse (n) the disappearance of the light of the sun or reflected light of the moon, when the moon is between the sun and the earth, or when the earth's shadow falls on the moon

estuary the mouth of a river

friar a man who is a member of a religious order

gale an extremely strong wind

gas mark a system for measuring temperature in a gas oven

generate to produce and send

get away from it all to escape from the noise and pressure of everyday life

heath area of sandy soil where you will probably find heather (a plant)

hull the main body of a ship

infamous well-known for negative reasons

lantern a light out-of-doors

legend a story or folk-tale

lighthouse-keeper the person who looks after the building with a light which warns ships

mainland a larger area of land in contrast to small islands

marsh wet land

medicine-man a doctor in primitive society

observe to watch carefully

offshore a short way out to sea

pastry a mixture of flour and water, used for pies

peninsula an area of land almost surrounded by sea

pirate a person who robs ships at sea

rear (v) to bring up an animal

recipe instructions for preparing and cooking food

rite/ritual religious act(s), usually performed in a special order

savoury not sweet, salty

shipwreck a ship which has been destroyed at sea, often on rocks

stalactite a long structure formed by dripping water which hangs from the roof of a cave

stalagmite like a stalactite, but it stands on the floor of a cave

suppressed stopped by the law

surf to ride on top of the waves, balanced on a long board

teaspoon a spoon used to stir tea

terrestrial of the earth or land

track a line or path

traffic jam a long queue of cars, lorries, buses, bicycles, etc

transatlantic steamer a large ship worked by steam which crosses the Atlantic Ocean

utensil a tool for use in the kitchen

washed up carried on to the beach by the waves of the sea

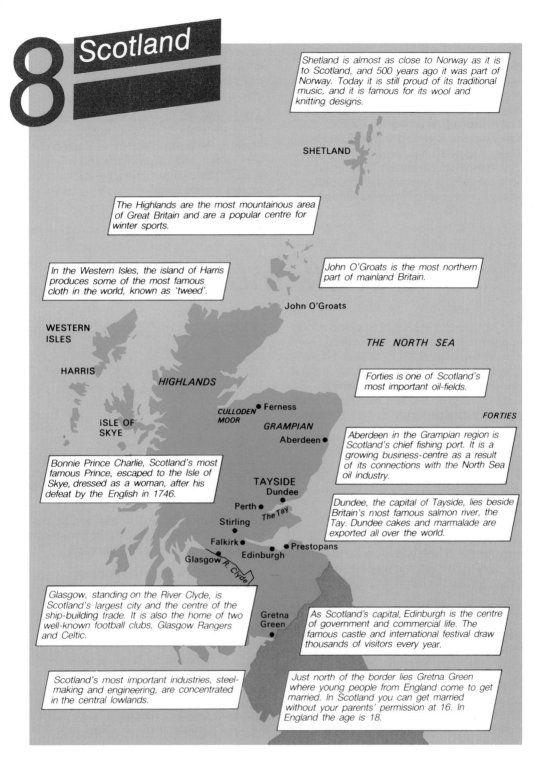

Shetland is almost as close to Norway as it is to Scotland, and 500 years ago it was part of Norway. Today it is still proud of its traditional music, and it is famous for its wool and knitting designs.

SHETLAND

The Highlands are the most mountainous area of Great Britain and are a popular centre for winter sports.

In the Western Isles, the island of Harris produces some of the most famous cloth in the world, known as 'tweed'.

John O'Groats is the most northern part of mainland Britain.

John O'Groats

WESTERN ISLES

THE NORTH SEA

HARRIS

HIGHLANDS

Forties is one of Scotland's most important oil-fields.

ISLE OF SKYE

CULLODEN MOOR ● Ferness

GRAMPIAN

Aberdeen ●

FORTIES

Aberdeen in the Grampian region is Scotland's chief fishing port. It is a growing business-centre as a result of its connections with the North Sea oil industry.

Bonnie Prince Charlie, Scotland's most famous Prince, escaped to the Isle of Skye, dressed as a woman, after his defeat by the English in 1746.

TAYSIDE
Dundee

Perth ●

The Tay

Stirling ●

Dundee, the capital of Tayside, lies beside Britain's most famous salmon river, the Tay. Dundee cakes and marmalade are exported all over the world.

Falkirk ● ● Prestopans

Glasgow ● R. Clyde Edinburgh

Glasgow, standing on the River Clyde, is Scotland's largest city and the centre of the ship-building trade. It is also the home of two well-known football clubs, Glasgow Rangers and Celtic.

Gretna Green

As Scotland's capital, Edinburgh is the centre of government and commercial life. The famous castle and international festival draw thousands of visitors every year.

Scotland's most important industries, steel-making and engineering, are concentrated in the central lowlands.

Just north of the border lies Gretna Green where young people from England come to get married. In Scotland you can get married without your parents' permission at 16. In England the age is 18.

At the beginning of the 6th century, Scotland was ruled by Scottish kings and queens, but was divided between different groups of people. The *Picts* and *Celts*, who were the oldest inhabitants, the *Scots*, who came from Northern Ireland, the *Britons*, who were driven north by the Anglo-Saxon invaders of England, and the *Angles*, who originally came from what is now Germany. The Romans had left two centuries earlier.

England and Scotland were finally united when, in 1603, the son of Mary Queen of Scots became James I of England. This was because Mary's cousin Elizabeth I of England had left no heir when she died. Today Scotland is part of the United Kingdom and is governed from London. There is a special minister in the Government, the Secretary of State for Scotland, who is responsible for education, local government and other important matters in Scotland. Although the legal, education and banking systems are slightly different from those in England, life is very similar to the rest of the United Kingdom.

All the inhabitants speak English although about 100,000 still speak Scottish Gaelic. Many of the Scottish accents of English are very strong, and visitors from abroad (or even England) sometimes have difficulty in understanding them!

Folk music

The McCalmans are one of Scotland's most popular folk groups. They have been playing together for a long time and have many fans both in Scotland and throughout the world. Their three-part harmony singing and good humour win them friends wherever they perform.

After studying at the Edinburgh College of Art they gave up their studies to follow their main interest, folk music.

When they were at college they began to learn the less well-known traditional songs and they still sing many of them today.

As well as singing, they play a variety of instruments. The guitar is of course one of the most important, but they also play the mandolin and the penny whistle.

Rise and Follow Charlie! is the title of one of the most popular songs the McCalmans sing. It dates from the time of the Jacobite rebellions when Scotland fought her last battle against the English.

In 1707 a special treaty united the governments of Scotland and England. The Protestant Church replaced the Catholic Church as the ruling church in Scotland.

However, many of the people who lived in the Highlands and Western Isles did not welcome this change. They still supported the grandson of the Catholic James II, who had been exiled in 1688. His name was

The McCalmans.

Prince Charles Edward Stewart and he was known as Bonnie Prince Charlie because he was young and handsome ('bonnie').

Charlie spent twenty years in Rome preparing to win back the Crown of Great Britain for his father and himself, and then returned to Scotland. The Highlanders were very proud that he still spoke Gaelic, and wore the traditional tartan kilt. In 1745, he landed in the Western Isles, then with 2,500 men, he marched south to Perth, Stirling and Edinburgh. There, on 17th September, his father was proclaimed king of Scotland and England. Four days later the Jacobites defeated the English army at Prestonpans.

On 1st November Charlie led his men as far south as Derby in England. However not as many Jacobite supporters joined them in England as they had hoped, and Charlie decided to retreat. The Jacobites returned

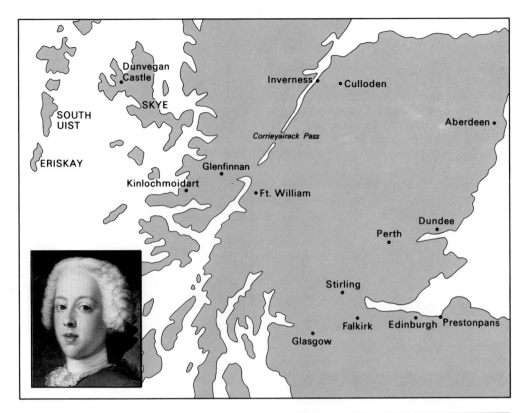

to Scotland on 21st December and defeated yet another English army at Falkirk on 17th January 1746. By April, however, the Duke of Cumberland had built up a huge army of 9,000 Protestant soldiers from England and Europe. On 16th April they met Charlie's army of 5,000 tired and hungry men in the wind and the rain at Culloden. There was a terrible and bloody battle and the Jacobites were defeated.

Charlie wandered in exile in the Scottish Highlands and in Europe. There was a reward of £30,000 for his capture but the Highlanders, though poor, never betrayed the man they loved so much.

After the rebellion of 1745, the Highlanders were forbidden to carry weapons, to speak their own language, Gaelic, or wear their own dress. Much of their land was sold by the British government.

ANSWER

Look at the map, and mark in Charlie's journey. Describe what happened at each place, and the date when it took place.

SING

There are many songs like the McCalmans' *Rise and Follow Charlie!* that tell Charlie's sad story. The best known is *Charlie is My Darling.*

Charlie is My Darling

CHORUS
Oh! Charlie is my darling,
My darling, my darling,
Oh! Charlie is my darling,
The young Chevalier.

'Twas on a Monday morning,
Right early in the year,
When Charlie came to our town,
The young Chevalier. Oh!　　　CHORUS

As he came marching up the street,
The pipes played loud and clear,
And the folk came running out,
To meet the Chevalier. Oh!　　　CHORUS

They've left their bonnie Highland hills,
Their wives and bairnies dear,
To draw the sword for Scotland's lord,
The young Chevalier. Oh!　　　CHORUS

Beating the 'Sassenachs'!

Relations between England and Scotland today are very good but sometimes there are problems at sporting events between the two countries. At the end of every football season England plays Scotland, and every two years the game is played at the famous Wembley Stadium in north London. Some

Londoners, however, are sure that the Scots have never really forgotten that terrible defeat at Culloden. They believe that the trip to London is part of the Scottish revenge on the 'sassenachs' – the Scottish name for the English or 'Anglo-Saxons'!

Scotland versus England.

N. Ireland versus Eire.

Although England, Scotland, Wales and Northern Ireland have their own national football teams, in the Olympic Games there is only one team that represents the United Kingdom. The athletes from the four countries work together as one team to win for Britain. If they win a medal, all four countries are equally proud. This means, of course, that it is very difficult for Britain to send a football team to compete in the Games!

Ian Rush (Wales).

TALKING POINT

English football fans have a very bad reputation in Europe for their behaviour.

What in your opinion causes football hooliganism, and how would you prevent it?

The Highland games

The games which are now celebrated in the Highlands first started in Celtic times and were always held in front of the king. Competitions were held to find the strongest and fastest men to be body-guards and messengers. Essential to the modern games are the events such as putting the stone, throwing the hammer and tossing the caber.

Other events include running and jumping, as well as competitions for playing the bagpipes and dancing traditional Highland dances.

The games held in the northeast are best known for the athletic events, whilst the best piping is traditionally found in the Highlands and Islands off the west coast.

Tossing the caber.

Tattoo spectacular

The Edinburgh military tattoo takes place every August and September, and is known throughout the world. For 90 minutes on five or six nights a week, 600 people perform under floodlights. They are surrounded on three sides by an audience of 9,000. On the fourth side is the castle itself which provides an exciting setting for the evening's performance of military music, marching and other spectacular displays.

The name tattoo has an interesting origin. Traditionally soldiers were told to return to the living-quarters each night by a beat of the drum which sounded like 'tat-too'. After this time the pubs would serve them no more whisky!

On the final night of the display the sky is filled with the bright colours of exploding fireworks.

WORDS

The athletic events at the Highland games are traditional, and not included in the modern Olympic games. What are the names of the different Highland events? Compare them with the athletic events at the Olympics.

Welcome to the Festival

At the same time as the tattoo, you can go to the famous Edinburgh festival. Since it started in 1947, the festival has had the aim of bringing to Scotland's capital the finest performers and productions from all over the world.

WHAT SHALL WE DO?

Look at this section from the first week's programme. Discuss what you want to do with a friend and make plans using the conversation to help you.

A What shall we do on Monday?
B How about going to a concert?
A O.K. What's on?
B Well, there's a piano concert on at The Queen's Hall.
A Fine. I'll see you outside just before it starts.
B O.K. at 10.45 then.

FIRST WEEK THEATRE

	Sun 21 Aug	Mon 22 Aug	Tues 23 Aug
Usher Hall Lothian Road	8.00 pm Philharmonia Orchestra Berg: Beethoven This concert will be televised	8.00 pm Academy of St Martin in the Fields Schubert: Mozart: Strauss	no performance
The Queen's Hall South Clerk Street ♿	no performance	11.00 am Cécile Ousset piano Debussy: Fauré: Brahms: Prokofiev	11.00 am Melos Quartet of Stuttgart Ravel: Caplet: Debussy
King's Theatre Leven Street **Playhouse Theatre** Greenside Place	no performance	7.30 pm (King's) Hamburg State Opera Zemlinsky Double Bill	7.30 pm (Playhouse) Hamburg State Opera Mozart Die Zauberflöte
Assembly Hall The Mound	7.00 pm Citizens' Company Glasgow The Last Days of Mankind	7.00 pm Citizens' Company Glasgow The Last Days of Mankind	7.00 pm Citizens' Company Glasgow The Last Days of Mankind
Church Hill Theatre Morningside Road	no performance	7.30 pm 221B	2.45 pm Vienna Lectures 7.30 pm 221B
The Castle ♿	no performance	9.00 pm Military Tattoo	9.00 pm Military Tattoo

A tragic queen

Prince's Street is Edinburgh's shopping centre and it runs parallel with the Royal Mile which goes from the Castle to Holyrood House. This is the residence of the Queen when she is in Edinburgh and it was also the scene of one of the most famous murders in Scottish history.

Mary Queen of Scots.

Mary Queen of Scots had been brought up in France, and returned to Scotland in 1561. She was a Catholic in a country that was becoming more and more Protestant. This meant that all her life she was involved in religious and political struggles.

Mary made many mistakes in her life. The first real one was her marriage to Henry Lord Darnley in 1565. He was handsome and ambitious but at the same time vain, self-indulgent and weak. Their love did not last. Darnley became suspicious of Mary's Italian secretary, David Rizzio. On 9th March 1566, while Mary and her friends were having supper at Holyrood House, Darnley and his friends broke into the dining room, dragged Rizzio outside and stabbed him to death. The spot where this took place can still be seen today.

Mary continued to live an unhappy life and was exiled for many years in England. Her cousin Elizabeth I of England had always been suspicious of her and decided that her worries would stop only when Mary was dead. Therefore, in 1587, she finally ordered that Mary should be executed.

Scotland seen from abroad

Caroline from
FRANCE

CAROLINE IGNARD, 20, of Chasseneuil, in south-west France, works as an au pair in Dundee, where she is also taking a course in English.

She hopes to go to university eventually and study English literature.

Said Caroline: "I love Scotland and the people I live with are very good to me.

"I am an only child. My parents live in a big house – in fact most people in our area own their own houses.

"I'm not very fond of Dundee – I prefer Edinburgh.

"The Scots are nice, though. As soon as they find out you're from France they become very friendly and helpful. They seem to like French people.

"Probably the biggest difference is in the weather. It's terrible here!"

Hans from
GERMANY

HANS-JOACHIM KOLL (24), who comes from Bonn, says: "I'm surprised by the lack of entertainment in a city as big as Glasgow.

"In Bonn, we've five theatres and about twenty discotheques for young people.

"Comparing the populations (Bonn has about 240,000 people) there's ten times as much to do in Bonn as there is in Glasgow. And your pubs close so early at night!

"Salaries in Germany are much higher than they are here. Young people have a lot more to spend than they do in Scotland."

TALKING POINTS

- Would you like to live in Scotland? What work would you do? What subject would you like to study at university? Why?
- Pubs close at 10.30p.m. or 11.00p.m. in Scotland. Do you think this is too early? Why?

TALKING POINT

The people of Ferness have to choose between their traditional way of life or a quick and easy profit! What advice would you give them?

Write down the advantages and disadvantages of the oil industry and decide on what would be the best thing for them to do.

LOCAL HERO

LOCAL HERO is a film made by Bill Forsyth, a writer and film director from Glasgow. Its story is quite simple. A big American Oil Company, Knox Oil, decides to build an oil refinery on the Scottish coast and sends a young executive to buy up the sleepy fishing village of Ferness. He expects to be met by strong opposition. Instead he finds the villagers very keen to sell their land in order to make a lot of money! They are all very angry with one old fool, the 'local hero' of the title, who won't sell his land.

"LOCAL HERO
is both a delightful and memorable experience
...I recommend you to see it..."
David Malcolm The Guardian

"Delightfully observed comedy"
David Castell Sunday Telegraph

"A magical brew of humour and enchantment...
a film to cherish for days...
probably years" *Richard Barkley Sunday Express*

"Funny, witty, gentle and loving"
Barry Norman Film 83

"Here is a British film rich in enchantment" *Arthur Thirkell Daily Mirror*

"A film with a loving heart and an exuberant charm" *Margaret Hinxman Daily Mail*

"I have only seen it twice and twice is not enough"
Michael Owen The Standard

Life on the rigs

Men working on the North Sea Oil rigs off Scotland's east coast can earn large salaries, but life can be very dangerous. Men work either for seven or fourteen days, with the same time back on land when they have finished their working period. At the end of each 12 hour day they normally return to their cabins, which are shared by two or four men. There is usually a lot for men to do in their free time with gymnasiums, video libraries, and a large supply of books all being available. The work is secure, and men earn enough money, almost £30,000 a year, to buy expensive homes in the attractive villages around Aberdeen. Many workers do not mind the long hours on the rigs because they have several days on-shore, which they can spend with their families. Alcohol is not normally allowed, and smoking is only permitted in some areas on the rigs.

However, there is always the risk of fire and on Wednesday 6th July 1988, the Piper Alpha oil rig, situated about 150 km. north-east of Wick in Scotland, blew up and caught fire immediately. Almost 190 men were killed in this tragedy, and there followed a large emergency rescue operation in the North Sea. Many workers jumped into the sea from the burning platform and were picked up by helicopters and small boats. The 100m. high platform was hit by an enormous explosion at about 9.30 p.m. and quickly caught fire. It is believed that the explosion was caused by a fault in one of the gas pipes. Piper Alpha was drilling for natural gas as well as oil. It took a long time before the fire was put out, and there were many problems in raising the damaged living quarters from the sea bed.

Many people are now worried about the safety of these oil platforms and the government has asked for a special report.

TRUE OR FALSE?

1 Men generally like working on the rigs.
2 There is very little to do during free time on the rigs.
3 Many of the workers live near Aberdeen.
4 The long hours on the rigs mean that men have longer periods at home with their families.
5 Piper Alpha pumped only oil.
6 The explosion happened just after lunch.
7 More than two hundred men were killed.
8 The government has closed down all the oil rigs.

(You will find the answers on page 139.)

PUZZLE

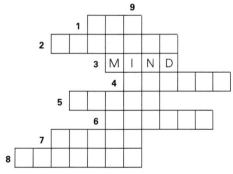

Read the text and complete the puzzle.
1 On the sea-_____.
2 _____ gas.
3 Men don't <u>mind</u> the long hours.
4 The damaged _____ quarters.
5 A _____ in the gas pipe.
6 Men were _____ up by helicopters.
7 Where the men sleep.
8 _____ is permitted in some areas.
9 The men are _____ for oil and gas.

(You will find the answers on page 139.)

Glasgow

Glasgow in the 1890s.

Background

Glasgow used to be called the 'dear dirty city', as its leading role during the industrial revolution of the nineteenth century caused a great deal of pollution. Standing on the River Clyde, 32 kilometres from the sea, it is the largest city in Scotland and the chief centre in the Strathclyde region. During the nineteenth century, its population increased almost ten times as people moved from the poorer Highlands and Islands to work in the expanding industries. Today, 800,000 people live there.

To allow the industries to grow during the nineteenth century, the River Clyde was widened. This allowed large ships from all over the world to sail into the heart of the city. Today many of the shipyards have closed and some traditional manufacturing industries have been replaced by the 'high-tech' electronics industries.

Although it used to be a very dirty river, the Clyde is now much cleaner. Recently, Scotland's most famous fish, the salmon, has been seen swimming once again in the heart of the city. Glaswegians themselves are discovering the beauty of their once filthy and overcrowded buildings through careful cleaning and restoration.

Perhaps because it has known so many hard times, it is one of the friendliest places in the world and is sometimes called 'the friendly city'.

The Arts

Glasgow is the home of the Scottish National Orchestra, the Scottish Opera and Scottish Ballet. These last two are based at the magnificent Theatre Royal. It has many smaller theatre companies, and the Kellingrove galleries contain the finest art collection in Britain outside London.

The Peoples' Palace, which was opened in 1898, has displays which try to reflect the lives of ordinary people. Not only are there memories of famous sportsmen and once popular theatres, but also sad reminders of life during the Industrial Revolution and records of those who tried to improve conditions for ordinary working people.

Glasgow in the 1980s.

The Theatre Royal, Glasgow.

WORDS

Find the eight words connected with shipping, which are hidden in the word circles. They may start anywhere and go clockwise or anti-clockwise.

① C A P T N I A

② A Y C H T

③ L I I A N S G

④ H R U A O R B

⑤ Y Q A U

⑥ C O E N A

⑦ R R E I V

⑧ R A G C O

(You will find the answers on page 139.)

Education

At secondary schools in Scotland, pupils may study as many as six subjects up to the age of eighteen. In England, usually only three subjects are studied during the last two years of school, the sixth form. Most Scottish Universities offer a four-year undergraduate degree course whereas, in England, the first degree course only lasts three years.

Three of its eight universities were founded in the fifteenth century, and a fourth in the sixteenth. They are thus much older than any of the English universities, other than Oxford and Cambridge.

Money

Although you can use the same money anywhere in the United Kingdom, only the Royal Bank of Scotland still prints one-pound notes.

James Watt (1736–1819)

It is said that James Watt developed his idea for the steam engine by watching a boiling kettle in his mother's kitchen and seeing how the steam pushed things out! He first became interested in machines, working as an ordinary mechanic at Glasgow University, which had been founded centuries before in 1451. His interest in the steam engine turned it into one of the most powerful and important machines in the Industrial Revolution.

Throughout his life, he could not stop inventing all kinds of machines, some of which were still being used earlier this century.

QUIZ

Who invented . . . ?
1 the electric battery
2 the telephone
3 the motor car
4 centigrade
5 the jet engine

(You will find the answers on page 139.)

The Highlands

The Scottish Highlands contain some of the most magnificent scenery in Europe, and the landscapes of northern Scotland form one of the truly 'wild' areas of Britain. Larger than East Anglia and the South-East of England put together, it is remarkable that the population is so small and concentrated in the towns. However, many of the places in the Highlands have not always been as deserted as they are today.

Many people left their small houses (called crofts) in the eighteenth and nineteenth centuries to find work in the large towns. But others were told to leave by cruel landlords who wanted to use their land for sheep-farming and deer-hunting. The old, the young and even the sick were thrown out of their homes. They had to move to the towns, go abroad or live in some of the newer villages on the Western Coast. They were not protected against these 'clearances' until a law was introduced in 1886.

Nowadays, 'crofters' may often have other part-time work, as well as looking after the land around their croft.

Whisky

A typical sight in many Highland valleys or glens are the white buildings of the malt whisky distilleries. No two malt whiskies are the same, and the taste cannot be copied anywhere else in the world, as the water comes from the local hills. Whisky was first produced in Scotland in 1494 and for many years there was a lot of smuggling to avoid paying taxes. There are more than 100 malt whisky distilleries in the Highlands and it is not surprising that the word 'Scotch' (Scottish is used to describe someone or something from Scotland) is used to mean whisky throughout the world.

TALKING POINT

Would you prefer to live in a town or in the country? Give five reasons for your choice.

WRITE

Write down as many diferent drinks as you can think of. How are they made?

Clans and tartans

The Gaelic word 'clann' means 'family' or 'descendants' and the great clans of the 16th and 17th centuries were indeed very similar to enormous families, ruled by powerful chiefs. Sometimes there were fierce battles between different clans but nowadays the MacDonalds and the MacKenzies, the Campbells and the Lindsays all live in peace with each other. It is possible to find people with these surnames in many English-speaking countries, and they all feel they share the same background.

The wearing of tartans or coloured checks was common in the Highlands before the defeat by the English in 1745. Originally, the tartan was worn as a single piece of cloth, drawn in at the waist and thrown over the shoulders. The kilt did not become popular until the beginning of the 18th century.

Each clan has its own tartan and, since the first international gathering of the clans in 1972, many more people have become interested in traditional forms of Scottish dress. Tartans are now part of international fashion. However, many visitors to Scotland are keen to find out if they have historical connections with any particular clan so that they may proudly wear the correct tartan.

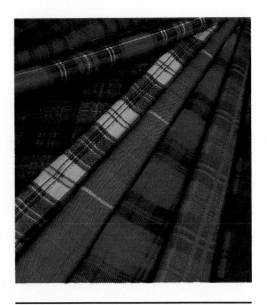

LOOK AND PRACTISE

Tartans are described as *coloured checks*.

Describe the clothes of your friends. Use these words to help you:

high-/low-/v-/round-necked
cotton, wool, silk, nylon, leather
plain, checked, striped, spotted
fashionable, old-fashioned
loose-/tight-fitting, casual, formal
pointed, round, short, long

TALKING POINT

What do you think of modern fashions? What clothes do you enjoy wearing? Give your reasons.

Scottish names

Many people in Scotland have the name MacDonald or MacKenzie. 'Mac' means 'son of' and people with this name usually feel they belong to the same family or clan. Campbell or Cameron are other common surnames. Common boys' names are Angus, Donald or Duncan, and girls' names are Morag, Fiona or Jean.

The names Jimmy and Jock are so common that many English people call a man from Scotland 'a Jimmy' or 'a Jock'!

Scottish festivals

Hogmanay

At midnight on 31st December throughout Great Britain people celebrate the coming of the new year, by holding hands in a large circle and singing this song:

> *Should auld acquaintance be forgot*
> *And never brought to mind*
> *Should auld acquaintance be forgot*
> *For the sake of auld lang syne.*
>
> *For auld lang syne, my dear,*
> *For auld lang syne*
> *We'll take a cup of kindness yet,*
> *For the sake of auld lang syne.*

'For auld lang syne' means 'in memory of past times' and the words were written by Scotland's most famous poet, Robert Burns. He wrote much of his poetry in the Scots dialect.

New Year's Eve is a more important festival in Scotland than it is in England, and it even has a special name. It is not clear where the word 'hogmanay' comes from, but it is connected with the provision of food and drink for all visitors to your home on 31st December. In addition, many people believe that you will have good luck for the coming year if the first person to enter your house after midnight is a 'tall dark stranger'. It is also thought lucky if this person brings a piece of coal and some white bread! Most Scots take part in a *ceilidh* (Gaelic for 'dance') on New Year's Eve and there is much dancing and singing until the early hours of the morning.

Burns' Night

25th January is celebrated all over the world by Scotsmen wherever they are, as it is the birthday of Robert Burns. As at hogmanay, a special meal of haggis, potatoes and turnip is eaten, washed down by lots of whisky! The haggis is carried into the dining room behind a piper wearing traditional dress. He then reads a poem written especially for the haggis!

Recipe for Haggis

8 ozs Sheep's liver
4 ozs of Beef Suet (fat)
Salt and pepper
2 onions
1 cup oatmeal

Boil the liver and onions in water for 40 minutes. Drain; and keep the liquid. Mince the liver finely, and chop the onions with the suet. Lightly toast the oatmeal. Combine all the ingredients, and moisten the mixture with the liquid in which the liver and onions were boiled. Turn into a greased bowl, cover with grease-proof paper and steam for 2 hours.

Scottish words

Many Scottish people still use some Scottish words when they speak English.

'Wee', meaning small, is often heard in such expressions as 'wee laddie' – small boy. 'A bonnie lass' is a pretty girl and a 'bairn' is a young child. If someone answers your questions with 'aye' they are agreeing with you: 'aye' means yes. Finally, if you are offered a 'wee dram' be careful: you'll be given some whisky to drink and you will probably have to drink it all in one go!

Glossary

accent (*n*) a way of pronouncing English
all in one go without taking a breath while drinking
auld old
background past, ancestry
bagpipes musical instrument with air stored in a bag held under the arm
ban (*v*) to forbid, stop
beat (*n*) the noise of the drum
behave oneself not to cause a disturbance
betray to be unfaithful to
bloody where many people are killed
break into to use force to enter a place
bring to mind to remember
build up to increase the number
the Crown the right to be king or queen
date from (*v*) to have existed since
draw (*v*) to attract
dress (*n*) national costume
execute to be killed on the orders of a government or judge
floodlights large lights used for lighting a big area
folk group a band which plays traditional music of a country (folk music)
heir someone who has the legal right to receive money or property or a title when someone dies
highlander a person who comes from or lives in the Scottish Highlands
hooliganism activity of hooligans: rough, noisy people who cause trouble by fighting and breaking things
Jacobite supporter of King James II
kilt a tartan skirt worn by men in the Scottish Highlands
loose not tight-fitting, large
mandolin a musical instrument with 6 or 8 metal strings and a rounded body

marmalade jam made of oranges
oatmeal ground oats used to make porridge and oatcakes
oil-field an area where petroleum is found
penny whistle a simple cheap musical pipe
piping playing the bagpipes
proclaim to make known officially
putting the stone a sport in which a heavy stone is thrown as far as possible
quarters the place where soldiers live while in the army
rebellion fighting against someone in power, usually a government
retreat (*v*) to go back
rise (*v*) to stand up, leave one's home
self-indulgent giving way to one's own desires very easily
setting surroundings, place where something happens
so long as if, on condition that
spot the exact place
stab (*v*) to push a knife into
suet animal fat used in cooking
three part harmony singing three voices singing together
tight-fitting fitting close to the body
toss the caber to throw a log of wood as far as possible
treaty an agreement
turnip a root vegetable
vain having a high opinion of one's looks
wander to go from one place to another without a real purpose
wash down to swallow liquid with something
we'll take a cup of kindness yet we'll drink to our friendship

Llanfairpwllgwyngyllgogerychwyrndrobwllllantysiliogogogoch: this is the longest place-name in the United Kingdom!

Caernarfon is the ancient capital of Wales, where the British monarch's eldest son is traditionally crowned Prince of Wales.

North Wales has several impressive castles built by English kings. Anglesey is flat, but the rest of the region is very mountainous.

Mid Wales is rather sparsely populated. Along the coast are many fishing ports. Welsh is the everyday language of much of the north and west, and Aberystwyth is the centre of Welsh education and learning.

St David is the patron saint of Wales. On 1st March, St David's Day, patriotic Welsh people wear a leek or a daffodil, both symbols of Wales.

Every year, an international eisteddfod is held in Llangollen. People come from all over the world to recite poetry, sing and dance in this colourful competition.

North of Cardiff lie the valleys. These are the heart of the Welsh coal and steel industries.

Swansea: an important container-port. Caerphilly has one of the biggest castles in Europe, including a famous leaning tower. It was built by the Normans to defend themselves against the Welsh.

South Wales is a region of contrasts. The industrial cities of Swansea, Cardiff and Newport are only a short journey away from sandy beaches and busy holiday resorts.

Cardiff, the modern capital of Wales, has a castle dating back to Roman times, and a modern shopping centre.

Map labels: ANGLESEY, Llanfair P.G., Caernarfon, Snowdon, Llyn Peris, Llangollen, Llangybi, Harlech, Aberystwyth, Laugharne, Tredegar, Rhymney, Ebbw Vale, Llanelli, Rhondda, Swansea, Caerphilly, Newport, Severn bridge, Cardiff, R. Taff

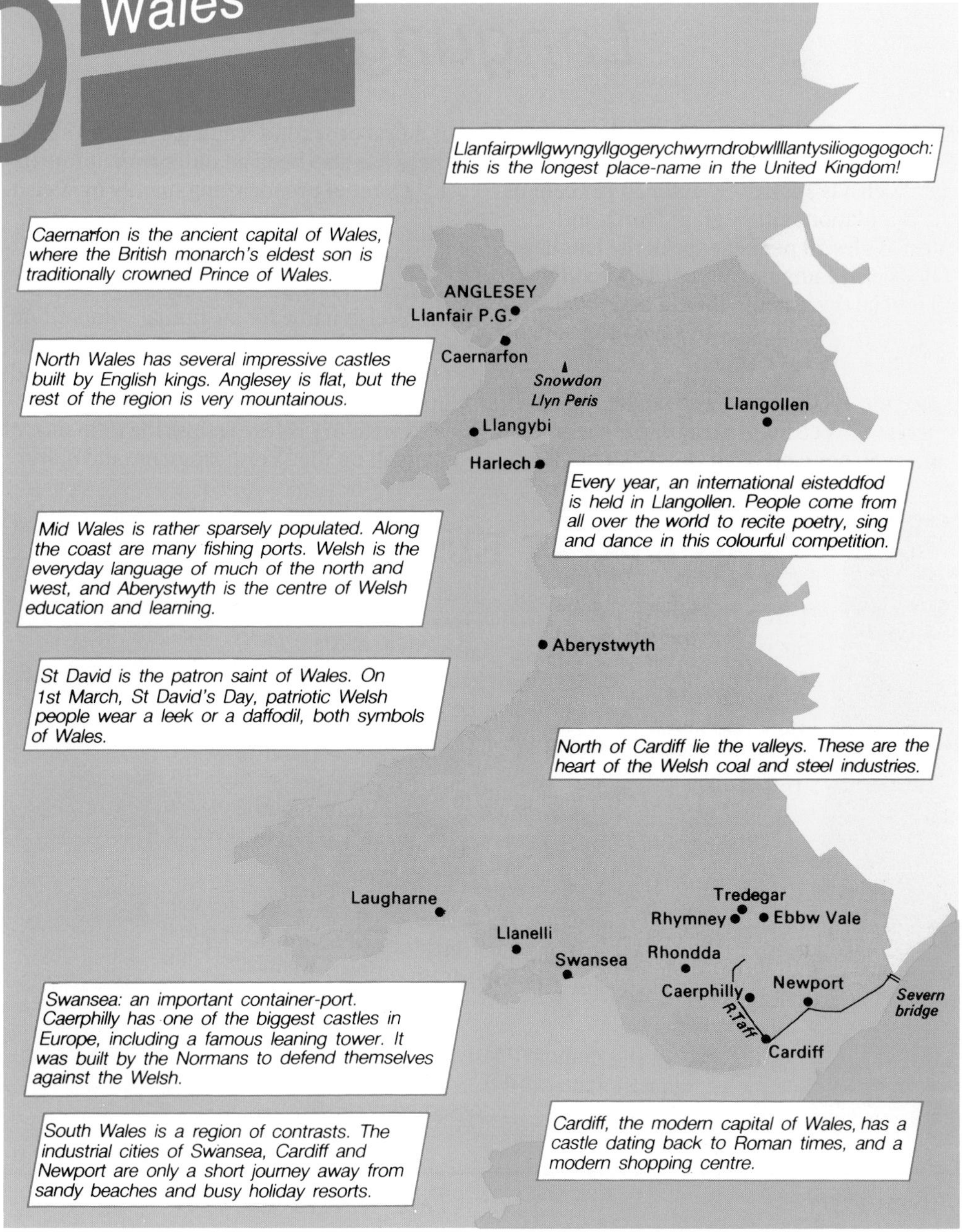

Wales is approximately 150 miles (242 km.) from north to south. About two-thirds of the total population of 2.8 million people live in the South Wales coastal area, where the three biggest towns are located: Swansea, Cardiff and Newport.

The Welsh are very proud of their language and culture. These are best preserved in the north and west of the country, for in the south and east they have been more challenged by industrialization. The west coast, mid Wales and North Wales are wild and beautiful!

Although visitors don't need passports to cross the border from England into Wales they soon realise that they are entering a country with its own distinct geography, culture, traditions and, of course, language.

Language

Welsh is one of the Celtic languages, like Scottish and Irish Gaelic. It is estimated that Welsh is spoken by 16 to 20 per cent of the population, although in North and West Wales 50 per cent speak the language. The Welsh Language Act of 1967 said that all official documents should be in both languages, and most road signs are printed in English and Welsh.

Since the 1960s there has been increased interest in Welsh. At secondary schools almost 50 per cent of all pupils learn Welsh as a first or second language. Since 1982 there has also been an independent fourth TV channel broadcasting mainly in Welsh.

Although not many Welsh words are well-known in England, the word *eisteddfod* is understood by almost everybody. This is the Welsh name for an annual competition where people meet to dance, sing and read poems. Usually, only Welsh is spoken and in recent years they have attracted people who wish to protest against the influence of English on the Welsh language and culture.

ARRESTS AT EISTEDDFOD

Three Welsh Language Society members were arrested at the National Eisteddfod yesterday as they demonstrated against English holiday homes in the region.

They rushed into the Welsh Office exhibition and threw paint at large pictures of Welsh castles. They decided these were suitable targets, as they had been built by English kings to keep down the Welsh.

According to the demonstrators, the Welsh Office has not done enough to prevent the growth of second homes in attractive areas. There are more than 18,000 holiday homes in Wales and people argue that the Welsh are unable to buy them because prices have risen so high. In this way the influence of the English visitors is weakening Welsh traditions.

The action by the demonstrators ignored a request from the organizers for young people to discuss problems rather than destroy property.

ANSWER

1 Why were the demonstrators arrested?
2 Why did they choose pictures of castles?
3 What were they protesting about?
4 How does the purchase of holiday homes in Wales affect the Welsh themselves?
5 How would the organizers of the *eisteddfod* prefer young people to express their protest?

TALKING POINTS

- Why do people get so angry about language? What can it represent?
- Some people argue that it would be a good idea if everybody in the world learnt a common language such as Esperanto. Do you agree?
- The organizers of the *eisteddfod* asked the young people to 'discuss problems rather than destroy property'. Is discussion *always* the best way to solve a problem?

History

To understand the feelings of the demonstrators, we should look briefly at the history of Wales.

The Celts who had first arrived in Wales in the 6th and 7th centuries BC were defeated by the invading Romans in 43 AD. The Romans also killed large numbers of Druids, the Celtic religious leaders, who had formed communites in the north and on the island of Anglesey.

In the 5th and 6th centuries AD many European saints travelled to Wales as Christian missionaries. Their names are remembered in some present-day Welsh place names. St Teilo and St Cybi are remembered by Llandeilo and Llangybi. *Llan* is the Welsh word for an area where a church stands.

The Saxons pushed the Welsh further and further towards the west until, in the 8th century, a Saxon king called Offa built a long ditch to keep them out of England! This ditch or dyke is 167 miles (269 km.) long and follows the line of much of today's border for most of the way. Then came the Normans who built enormous castles to protect themselves from attack from the west. Caerphilly Castle, 6 miles (10 km.) north of Cardiff, was one of the strongest in Europe. Even Oliver Cromwell, during the English Civil War, was unable to blow it up!

The Welsh fought for many years to win back their freedom. The Welsh king, Llewellyn the Great, tried to unite his people against the English, but his grandson, Llewellyn the Last, was finally defeated in 1282. The English built great castles at Harlech and Caernarfon, and in 1301 Edward I of England made his eldest son Prince of Wales. This tradition has been kept until the present day and in 1969 a similar ceremony took place again. The present Queen made her eldest son, Charles, Prince of Wales at Caernarfon castle.

In 1536 Henry VIII brought Wales under the English parliament through a special law. He insisted on the use of English for official business, but at the same time he gave the Welsh the freedom which the English already enjoyed. Since the 16th century Wales has been governed from London and in 1978 the Welsh voted by a large majority against a separate Welsh Parliament. In today's Government there is a special department and minister for Welsh affairs.

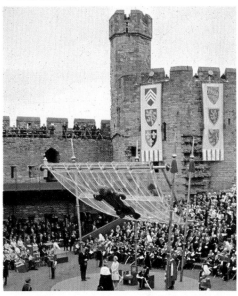

Caernarfen Castle, 1969 – A new Prince of Wales.

Princess Diana being greeted by children in Wales.

Life in the Valleys

A typical South Wales mining town, around 1910.

Mining has been one of the great Welsh industries for many years along with the iron and steel trades.

During the industrial revolution of the 18th and 19th centuries, the valleys of South Wales became the iron and steel capital of the world. The small villages that grew up around the pits and steel works developed their own special character. When people speak of life in the valleys they are usually thinking of a particular Welsh way of life where families stay very close together and villagers are very proud of their traditions. In particular the valleys are famous for producing male voice choirs, and rugby-players.

The Rhymney and the Rhondda are two of the best-known South Wales valleys. Standing high on the hillsides, you can look down and see the lines of terraced houses on the riverbanks. Some pits are now open to the public so that visitors can see for themselves just what the life of a miner is like.

The Welsh national game

Rugby Union is the national game of Wales, and during the 1970s the Welsh team was thought to be the best in the world. The rules of the game are rather complicated but mainly involve the carrying of an egg-shaped ball over your opponents' line and pressing it firmly on the ground to score a *try*. A team consists of fifteen players, eight of whom are usually much bigger and heavier than the rest. Their job is to win the ball so that the *three-quarters* can run forward over the line, trying to avoid the *tackles* of the opposing team. Often the heavier *forwards* can be seen pushing together in a *scrum*, trying to kick the ball backwards. Although the game seems to be similar to American football, the players are not allowed to throw the ball forward. Other points can be won by kicking the ball between the special 'H'-shaped goal-posts.

When the Welsh side are playing at home at *Cardiff Arms Park* their supporters often try to encourage them to play better by singing the Welsh National anthem, *Land of My Fathers*. The sound of thousands of Welsh voices singing this famous song usually helps the Welsh side to score another try to win the game. Naturally they are especially pleased when this is against the English!

PRACTISE

Describe the rules of any games that you know. Say what the players *have to do* to score points and what they *are not allowed to do*.

LOOK AND PRACTISE

You want to buy a house. Which house would you like to live in?

Many British people own their own houses. A *detached* house stands on its own, whilst *semi-detached* houses are built in pairs. *Terraced* houses are built in rows. If many houses are built in a new part of a town, this is called a *housing estate*.

1 **SMALL** terraced cottage in good decorative order.

2 **MODERN** four-bedroomed detached house, on large estate.

3 **SEMI-DETACHED** three storey older-style property, in need of some repair.

4 **BUNGALOW** with large garden.

5 **MODERN** terraced house for first-time buyers. A bargain.

6 **SEMI-DETACHED** three bedroomed family houses. Newtown estate.

The Welsh and their words

The traditional culture in Wales has always placed special emphasis on the reading of poetry and the singing of choirs. In the 19th century there was a powerful puritan religious movement that preached a good and simple life. In the chapels the oratory of the preacher and the strong singing of male voice choirs were used to win the hearts of the people and turn them away from bad living.

Politicians

This Welsh understanding of the power of words lies behind a fine tradition of radical and eloquent politicians who have contributed a great deal to British politics since the beginning of the century. David Lloyd George, although born in Manchester of Welsh parents, was brought up in Wales. He entered the House of Commons at the age of twenty-seven as a member of the Liberal Party.

After holding various government offices, he became the first Welsh Prime Minister of the United Kingdom in 1916, a post he held until 1922. His interest in the old and the poor led him to start the first national insurance scheme and system of old-age pensions. These were the foundation of the present day National Health Service and other forms of social welfare.

David Lloyd George.

Equally inspired by fairness and justice, Aneurin Bevan, who had worked in the coal-mines of South Wales as a boy, became one of the most powerful speakers ever known in the House of Commons. His battle with authority began when he led the miners in the general strike of 1926. He stood for Parliament as an independent Labour candidate in 1929 and by 1931 was the official Labour MP. During the Second World War he was famous for his long and bitter arguments with Winston Churchill about matters of government policy and defence. In 1948, as Minister of Health in the new Labour Government, he established the National Health Service to ensure that both rich and poor have the same health care. His commitment to the poor, together with his willingness to debate every issue with the opposition party, inspired many post-war Labour MPs.

Aneurin Bevan.

His successor in the constituency of Ebbw Vale was Michael Foot, who, although he never became Prime Minister, is famous for his speeches in the House of Commons and for his role as Minister of Employment in the Labour governments of the 1970s. His role as leader of the Labour party was taken over in 1983 by Neil Kinnock, another radical Welshman. He was born in Tredegar, the same village as Aneurin Bevan, and would be happy to think he was carrying on the same political tradition.

Like other Welsh politicians in the Labour party, he is against a separate Parliament for Wales. Plaid Cymru, the Welsh Nationalist Party, was very angry when he voted against this in 1978. Like Foot and Bevan before him, his roots lie firmly with the ordinary people of the Welsh valleys, and he feels that separate government would not really help them a great deal.

ANSWER

1 For how many years was Lloyd George Prime Minister?
2 What is he best remembered for?
3 What was Aneurin Bevan's most important contribution to British politics?
4 Why were Welsh Nationalists angry in 1978?

TALKING POINTS

● Should the Government of a country be responsible for health care or should there be some form of private insurance? If you can pay, should you be first in the queue for special medical treatment?
● Wales voted against having its own separate Parliament. Why do you think this happened? Are there any regions in your own country that would like their own government?

A poet

Dylan Thomas was born in Swansea and worked in London as a journalist writing radio and film scripts at the same time. One of his most famous radio plays, *Under Milk Wood*, has been adapted for the stage and performed all over the world. It creates the atmosphere of a typical Welsh village by the magical use of words and characters. Much of his working life was spent in such a village, Laugharne near Swansea on the South Wales coast. After a very troubled career, held back by his drinking, he died an early death in New York at the age of 39. The power of his poetry lies in its music and use of striking images.

One of his most famous poems begins with the lines opposite, which he wrote sitting beside the bed of his dying father.

Do not go gentle into that good night,
Old age should burn and rave at close of day,
Rage, rage against the dying of the night . . .

What's in a name?

The way in which British surnames have developed is very complicated. Before the Normans arrived, the use of surnames wasn't really known. Many English surnames were originally connected with a person's job – Charles *Baker*, Margaret *Thatcher*; someone's size – Jack *Long*, Mary *Little*; or a family relationship – Robin *Williamson* (Robin, son of William) Peter *Richardson*.

The most common Welsh surnames were all originally Christian names in some form: Dylan *Thomas*, Roger *Davies* (a form of David), Geoffrey *Jones* (from John), David *Williams* etc. Many other names come from the tradition of calling a child 'son of' his father using the Welsh word *ap* (or *ab*). This 'p' can be found at the beginning of many common Welsh names, eg Gary *Pritchard*, which is the same as the English *Richardson*. Other examples are *Prees*, *Price*, *Parry*, and *Pugh*.

Welshmen living in England are often called by the nickname 'Taffy'. This may come from the River Taff, which runs through the capital Cardiff, or it may come from *Dafydd*, the Welsh form of David.

WORDS

Divide these names into boys' and girls' Christian names, and surnames. Some names will fit more than one category.

> Ruth, Thomas, Smith, Julia, Rogers, Gemma, Abbot, Ian, Michael, Kenneth, James, Tracy, Teresa, Angela, Robinson, Price, Robert, MacGregor, Marilyn, April, Andrew, Felicity, Mark, Martin, Frederick, Peters, Gillian

Now look at the following names. They are not spelt correctly. Write them out correctly and divide them into boys' and girls' names. The first letter is always correct.

> Ezilatehb, Nglie, Gegoer, Ssanu, Algnae, Reotrb, Daina, Mnoiac, Peret.

(You will find the answers on page 139.)

'Fish and chips' comes into Welsh

Welsh is a Celtic language, and is very difficult to learn. It has very musical intonation, and difficult sounds such as *ch* and *ll*.

Because many people in Wales speak English, the Welsh language has borrowed a lot of English words. Many Welsh-speakers going out to buy the most famous British meal would ask for 'fish and chips i swper' (for supper).

Parts of the motor-car such as 'clutch', 'brake' or 'radiator' have come into Welsh almost unchanged.

Many Welsh-speakers use English words and add a Welsh ending, so we hear 'switchio', 'climbio', and 'recommendio'.

Some people think that this is lazy and that new words should be properly translated into Welsh before being used.

TALKING POINTS

- Are there English or other foreign words used in your own language? Why are they used?
- Do you think people should use English words without translating them?

The National Parks

The engine of the Snowdon mountain railway sometimes drives backwards!

There are three National Parks in Wales which cover approximately one-fifth of the whole country. These parks are protected by law because of their natural beauty, but ordinary people still live and work there. The most famous of the parks is Snowdonia in the north-west. It covers 840 square miles (2,176 sq. km.) of some of Wales' most breathtaking countryside. The highest mountain range in Wales is in this area, with several peaks over 3,000 feet (910 m.). The highest, Snowdon, is 3,560 feet (1,085 m.).

You can reach the summit on foot or by the Snowdon mountain railway, which is 4.5 miles (7 km.) long.

Many people travel to the parks each year for special holidays. These include a large number of outdoor activities such as walking, climbing, and riding, or water-sports such as canoeing and fishing. People camp and live without all the usual comforts of home.

PRACTISE

You have planned a camping holiday in Snowdonia and are deciding what you should take with you. Here is a possible list of equipment:

sleeping bag	reading material
rucksack	map
pillow	towel
soap	matches
guidebook	extra pair of shoes
toothbrush	insect-repellent
toothpaste	scissors
cooking pan	torch (flashlight)
penknife	extra money
string	dictionary
food for 3 days	compass
extra set of clothes	pen
camera	tin opener
	water

Which items would be useful and which could you manage without? Decide which ten items you consider most important and give your reasons.

WRITE

You have been on holiday in North Wales for a week now and have written this postcard to some English friends. Some words are missing. Choose them from the list given and write in the address in the correct order.

Dear ----,
I thought I ---- send you a card to ---- you know how I ----. The weather has been ----.
It has rained ---- every day! But we are having lots of ----, canoeing and ----. I hope to see you next ----.
All the ----,

---- ----

Lexdon Road	let
walking	am
week	almost
Max Greene	Colchester
England	19
fun	CO3 9DW
terrible	Essex
would	Max
best	

Energy inside a Welsh mountain

From the top lake . . .

. . . the water turns the turbines to produce electricity.

From the bottom lake, the water is pumped back up the mountain.

One of the biggest power-stations in the world is being built in the heart of a Welsh mountain. It uses neither oil nor coal to produce electricity, but the water of a large mountain lake.

In a few thousand years people may discover the machines and wonder what had been happening there. Chief engineer Bill Thompson says that some may think that it was a church. Certainly the large mountain caves remind us of a magnificent cathedral, especially when they are quiet. However, they are usually full of noise: vehicles thundering through the dark tunnels, the noise of pumps, hammering and shouting.

The underground pumped power station is the largest in Europe and is used to produce electricity by pumping water again and again between two lakes. The water is let out through the bottom of the top lake, Machlyn Mawr, and then it passes down to drive the turbines inside the mountain. The water turns the turbines which produce electricity. Afterwards the water is collected in the bottom lake, Llyn Peris, at the foot of the mountain in the heart of Snowdonia. The turbines then change direction and work as pumps, returning the water to the top lake, ready to be used again.

TALKING POINTS

- People often speak of the 'energy crisis' because the world may be running out of energy. What do you think are the best ways of using coal, oil, gas and electricity more efficiently?
- What other forms of energy could people use – for example, solar power, wind and wave power, nuclear power?
- Is nuclear power the best way to solve the energy crisis?

Cardiff: a modern capital

Cardiff Town Hall.

Cardiff has been the official capital of Wales since 1955. There has been a community here for hundreds of years, but it began to grow quickly and to become prosperous during the nineteenth and early twentieth centuries. This was the period when the coal, iron and steel industries were developing in South Wales, and Cardiff became a major industrial town and an important port. However, when these industries began to decline, Cardiff suffered too. Today, the docks are much smaller, but the city is now expanding as a commercial and administrative centre. It is an attractive and interesting place to live in, with good communications, plenty of parks and a varied population which includes nearly 10,000 university and college students.

As a tourist, you might want to visit the castle and Llandaff cathedral, or the National Museum of Wales. If you like music, there is the famous national concert hall, St David's Hall, or the New Theatre, which is the home of the Welsh National Opera Company.

WRITE

Re-write these sentences in the correct order to form a paragraph about the history of Cardiff.

1 It expanded suddenly during the nineteenth century into a great port.
2 A community has existed here for nearly 2,000 years.
3 During the Middle Ages, it was a small market town.
4 In AD76, the Romans reached Cardiff and built a stronghold.
5 When these industries declined, Cardiff became less prosperous too.
6 Happily, after a difficult period, the city is now prospering once again.
7 Not much is known after this until the Normans arrived in 1091.
8 This was because of the development of coal and other industries in South Wales.

(You will find the answers on page 139.)

WORD GAME

First find the answers to these clues. Then take the first letter of each answer and re-arrange them to find the name of another Welsh city. The answers are in the text.

1 If you were born in Cardiff, you would be this. _ _ _ _ _

2 You can see the Welsh National Opera here.

_ _ _   _ _ _ _ _ _ _

3 This adjective describes Cardiff.

_ _ _ _ _ _ _ _ _ _

4 Cardiff is the

_ _ _ _ _ _ _ _ _ _ _ _ _ _

centre of Wales.

5 This was once an important industry in South Wales. _ _ _ _ _

6 You can go to the theatre or to a concert in the _ _ _ _ _ _ _

7 10,000 people do this in Cardiff.

_ _ _ _ _

The name of the city is

_ _ _ _ _ _ _

(You will find the answers on page 139.)

A student in Wales

After London, the University of Wales is the largest university in the United Kingdom. It was established almost one hundred years ago and incorporated three existing colleges at Aberystwyth, Bangor and Cardiff. Since then, colleges at Swansea and Lampeter have also become part of the same university, together with the College of Medicine and the Institute of Science and Technology in Cardiff. Because of its size, the university is able to offer a wide range of courses, and students can choose the location they prefer. Each college has a separate identity and character. St David's College Lampeter is in the middle of beautiful countryside; Aberystwyth is on the coast; Bangor is on the edge of the mountainous region of Snowdonia, and Swansea and Cardiff are in an urban environment.

The table contains more information about each of the University Colleges.

TALKING POINT

Discuss with a partner which University College you would like to study at. Give reasons, using information from the table and from the text.

University College	Population of town	Student population	Male/Female ratio	Special courses	Leisure activities Additional information
Aberystwyth	11,000	3,245	♂ 53% ♀ 47%	Geology Celtic Studies Education	Tourist town. Sports hall, swimming pool, National Library of Wales, theatre, art gallery, concert hall.
Bangor	12,000	2,903	♂ 55% ♀ 45%	Engineering Ocean Sciences	Small town. Sports centre. Water sports, rock climbing. Near Snowdonia.
Cardiff	300,000	8,217	♂ 53% ♀ 47%	Medicine Law EEC Studies	Cosmopolitan city. Shopping centres, concert halls, theatres, etc. Good communications.
St David's	4,000	744	♂ 46% ♀ 54%	History Theology Welsh Studies	Small market town. Walking, pony trekking.
Swansea	187,000	4,750	♂ 58% ♀ 42%	Natural Sciences Geography	Large, industrial city. Sport and leisure facilities. Close to lovely countryside. Good communications.

WORD SEARCH

In the square below, six words are hidden. They are all hobbies you could start at the University of Wales.

A	L	P	B	O	C	A	R
T	S	R	A	C	L	T	I
H	E	A	N	L	I	S	D
E	W	K	I	X	M	G	I
A	N	F	U	L	B	K	N
T	S	I	N	G	I	N	G
R	U	G	B	Y	N	N	W
E	H	N	D	L	G	O	G

(You will find the answers on page 139.)

WRITE

Write a letter to one of the colleges asking for information about courses for overseas students.

Books, books, books!!!
Hay-on-Wye is a Welsh border town on the southern bank of the River Wye. It is unique, because although its total population is only 1,000, it has fourteen bookshops which contain well over a million antiquarian and second-hand books. In fact, it is the largest second-hand book-selling centre in the world. One of the most amazing shops is a converted cinema. This alone has more than a quarter of a million books for sale. Hay-on-Wye is the ideal holiday centre for bookworms!

WORD GAME

How many words can you make from the letters of Shakespeare? (There are at least 25.)

Big Pit Mining Museum

Coal mining has played a very important part in the lives of generations of people living in South Wales. For this reason, the Mining Museum at Blaenavon has re-created the atmosphere of a working mine of the past, to give visitors a taste of what life was like for miners in the 'old days'. On the surface, you can see such things as a typical miner's cottage and the pithead baths. For the underground tour, visitors have to wear safety helmets and cap lamps. They are taken down a shaft 100 metres deep in a pit cage, and are shown the coal faces, underground stables and workshops by ex-miners.

Here is some information for people wishing to visit the museum.

- Open April to end of October, Tuesday to Sunday from 10.00.
- Closed on Mondays, except Bank Holidays.
- The last complete tours start at 3.30.
- If you are going on the underground tours, you must wear strong shoes and warm clothing.
- Children under the age of eight are not allowed underground.
- Cafeteria where you can buy hot food and drinks.
- Souvenir shop.
- Party bookings, by arrangement, November to March. Discounts available.

TRUE OR FALSE?

According to the information, are the following statements true or false?

1 You cannot visit Bit Pit during the winter.
2 The museum closes at 3.30.
3 Special prices are available, if you go with a group.
4 You will need to take your own food.
5 The museum is not usually open on Mondays.
6 You do not need to wear special clothes.
7 Very young children are not allowed to go on the underground tours.

(You will find the answers on page 139.)

Glossary

breathtaking something so beautiful that it stops you breathing for a moment

bungalow a small house with just one storey

channel a TV station

clutch a pedal to connect and disconnect the gear

common language a language spoken by everybody

container-port a port dealing with cargo in very large special containers

demonstrate to protest publicly

distinct separate and special

ditch a long hole dug in the ground

eisteddfod annual gathering of poets and musicians in Wales

eloquent speaking well and fluently

Esperanto an artificial language designed for world use

estate an area on which many houses are built

hammer (*v*) to hit repeatedly

hold office to have various jobs in government

insect repellent a cream or spray which kills insects

inspired influenced

leek a long onion-like vegetable

manage without to live without, ie leave behind

national anthem the song of a country

National Health Service the organization which gives free health care to all citizens

national insurance money taken by the government from one's pay, which acts as insurance in case of sickness, unemployment etc

old-age pension money received by people over 60 when they stop work

oratory the skill of making persuasive, emotional speeches

own (*v*) to possess, have as property

patriotic strongly supporting one's own country

peak (*n*) the top of a mountain

pit (*n*) a hole in the ground where miners dig out coal

Plaid Cymru Welsh Nationalist Party

preserved kept pure, unchanged by outside influences

radical wanting political change

rage (*v*) to be very angry

rave (*v*) to behave as if mad

roots feeling of sharing a common past, culture etc

rucksack a bag carried on the back

script the text for a radio or TV play

social welfare social services financed by the government; health care, pensions, insurance, dole, etc

solar of the sun

stand for Parliament to offer oneself for election

strike (*n*) a time when workers refuse to work, in order to get better pay and conditions

striking images ideas or pictures in poetry that are unusual and wild

summit the top of a mountain

tackle to attack an opponent, in order to take the ball in rugby

target something to be hit

thunder (*v*) to make a noise like thunder in a storm

try (*n*) (rugby) touching down the ball behind the opponents' goal-line

turbine an engine whose driving-wheel is turned by water

whale a large sea animal

Rathlin Island is inhabited by only thirty families. For centuries the Scots and Irish fought over the island but eventually the Irish were allowed to stay because of the absence of snakes on the island. (It is said that St Patrick drove all the snakes out of Ireland!)

The county of Londonderry has fine beaches in the north and the Sperrin Mountains in the south. The county town, Londonderry, is one of the two most important cities in Northern Ireland.

RATHLIN ISLAND

Giant's Causeway

The Antrim coast is a remarkable stretch of country. Its geological composition goes back 300 million years!

• Londonderry

LONDONDERRY

COUNTY ANTRIM

DONEGAL

Sperrin Mountains

TYRONE

Lough Neagh

• Belfast

U L S T E R

Lough Erne

COUNTY DOWN

Enniskillen •

FERMANAGH

ARMAGH

• Downpatrick

MONAGHAN

Mourne Mts.

CAVAN

Fermanagh is almost as much lake as land, with huge Lough Erne running through its centre. Enniskillen is the county town.

EIRE

County Down is one of the best farming counties in Ireland. It is closely associated with St Patrick, Ireland's patron saint, after whom the county town of Downpatrick is named. In the south of the county are the Mourne Mountains.

Armagh was important long before Christianity as the home of Ulster kings for six centuries. The north of the county is a rich fruit-producing area.

The province of Northern Ireland (sometimes called 'Ulster') consists of six counties: Antrim, Down, Armagh, Tyrone, Fermanagh and Londonderry. Belfast is the capital city. The province is surrounded by sea to the north and east, by the Republican counties of Donegal to the west and Cavan and Monaghan to the south.

The troubles

The 'Peace Line' between Catholic and Protestant Belfast.

When trouble started in Northern Ireland in the late 1960s it took many people by surprise. However the violence and suffering which Northern Ireland has been experiencing are simply the latest events in an old story which began long ago.

Reformation and Plantation

The history of Anglo-Irish relations began with the colonization of Ireland by the Normans under Henry II of England in the 12th century. Over the next two centuries these Norman settlers became 'more Irish than the Irish', and it is possible that Ireland might have ended up as a contented Anglo-Irish society under the British Crown. However, in the 16th century Henry VIII quarrelled with Rome and declared himself head of the Anglican Church. Resistance from Irish Catholics was strong but was put down by Henry's armies. And so by trying to force Irish Catholics to become Anglican and by taking a lot of their land, Henry began the two lasting problems of Anglo-Irish relations – religion and land.

What he started was continued by his daughter Elizabeth I. Ulster was a specially difficult area to bring under her rule. The soldiers of the province of Ulster successfully fought against Elizabeth's armies until 1603, but were finally defeated. Then the 'Plantation of Ulster' began. 'Plantation' meant that twenty-three new towns were built in Ulster to protect the needs of 170,000 new, Protestant settlers known as 'planters', most of whom came from Scotland. This policy of plantation soon changed the structure of society in Ulster.

Religion separated the planters and native Irishmen. The Scots planters were Presbyterians, a form of Protestantism, and they were deeply suspicious of Catholics and Catholicism. But they brought with them their own laws and customs relating to land, which encouraged greater social stability and economic growth. The Scots also placed great emphasis on education and hard work, and they were good at business. All this sowed the seeds of Ulster's 19th century industrialization, which made it different from the rest of Ireland.

ANSWER

1. What do you think is meant by 'the troubles'?
2. Who were the Normans?
3. Why did Irish Catholics dislike Henry VIII?
4. Who were the 'planters'?
5. How did plantation change the structure of Ulster society?
6. In what way did Ulster become different from the rest of Ireland during the 19th century?

Cromwell and William of Orange

During the Civil War in England, things became even worse in Ireland. A Catholic army was formed there in support of the king, Charles I, but Cromwell's Puritan (Protestant) force of 20,000 men was too strong for them. Cromwell's army not only defeated the Catholic, royalist army but also killed many civilians as well. This caused more bitterness between Protestant and Catholic, planter and native.

Forty years later there was again Irish support for the deposed Catholic king, James II, but in 1690 the Protestant forces of William of Orange (William III) finally defeated the Catholics led by James at the Battle of the Boyne.

Famine

No event in Irish history has had a deeper effect on Irish national feeling than the Great Famine of 1845–9. In the 19th century most of the Irish depended on agriculture – indeed, most of them depended on simple potato-farming for their survival. The poor peasants made their living from tiny pieces of land and had to pay high rents for this land. Potatoes were their main food and when the potato harvest was bad for four years in succession, there was a terrible famine in the country.

The Great Famine left one million people dead and forced another million to emigrate to the United States of America. It also left bitter feelings towards the British Government because they had not done enough to help the poor people during the famine.

Although these events took place three hundred years ago, they are still remembered in Ulster today. The Protestants still call themselves Orangemen and annually celebrate William's victories over the Catholics with parades and banners. The bitterness of history is kept alive in Northern Ireland.

TALKING POINTS

- There are still parts of the world where thousands, even millions, of people are hungry and even die of starvation. Do you know any places where this is happening?
- Do the rich nations of the world do enough to help poor countries?
- Can an individual do anything to help someone who is starving on the other side of the world?

NO SURRENDER

1688

THE PROTESTANT RELIGION I WILL MAINTAIN

DERRY AUGHRIM AND THE BOYNE

WILLIAM III. PRINCE OF ORANGE

Landing of King William III. at Carrickfergus.

Shall Ulster freemen e'er be slaves?
No! Rather be its soil their graves.

Two nations?

Some people say that from the time of the famine the gradual appearance of two nations can be seen in Ireland. During the 19th century Ulster, and particularly Belfast, became industrialized in a similar way to the North of England. Because of its industrial economy Ulster was not as badly affected by the poor potato harvest as the rest of Ireland, which depended on agriculture. Also, the land laws in Ulster were much fairer than in the rest of Ireland. This meant that, whereas people in the south of Ireland blamed British rule for their poverty and suffering, the people of Ulster found that union with Britain had brought them prosperity, and markets for their industrial products.

During the attempts between 1886 and 1914 to get Home Rule for Ireland (independence from Britain in all things relating to internal affairs), the people of Ulster resisted strongly and said they would fight rather than give up union with Britain.

PUZZLE

Find the six words ending in '-ation' and discover the word made by the letters in the boxes. There are clues to help you.

CLUES
1 Number of people living in a country or area.
2 The settling of people in a new country which is governed by the mother country.
3 The introduction of machines and factories in the 19th century.
4 The settling of Protestants from the British mainland in Ulster.
5 Movement which protested against the Catholic church.
6 Extreme hunger.

(You will find the answers on page 139.)

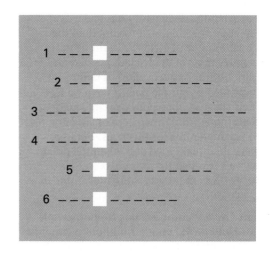

Partition

After a long and violent struggle, the southern part of Ireland finally became a Free State in 1921. Ulster chose to remain part of the United Kingdom of Great Britain and Northern Ireland. This division of Ireland is known as 'partition'.

The Irish Free State declared itself a republic in 1949 and is now known as the Irish Republic, or Eire (an old Irish word for Ireland). It is completely separate and independent from Britain and Northern Ireland, and its government is in the capital city, Dublin.

In 1949, Northern Ireland still had its own Prime Minister and its own Parliament at Stormont in Belfast which was responsible for the province's internal (not foreign) affairs, but it was still part of the UK.

Conflict

From the beginning, the Stormont Parliament was dominated by Protestants. Northern Irish Catholics, who were now in a minority, found that they did not have equal opportunities with Protestants for housing and employment. A campaign of civil rights for Catholics was started but very little attention was paid to it by the ruling Protestants.

In 1969 there was rioting in Northern Ireland between Catholics and Protestants. By 1972 the hostility between the two groups was so bad that Britain suspended the Northern Irish Parliament at Stormont and sent in the British army to keep the peace. The soldiers were welcomed at first by the Catholics as protectors from Protestant violence, but when the army began house-to-house searches of Catholic areas for men with guns, the welcome soon turned to bitterness.

There have been many deaths since 1969. In 1972, on what became known as 'Bloody Sunday', British soldiers opened fire on Catholic demonstrators in Londonderry and thirteen people were killed. In addition, many British soldiers have been killed. Both the Protestant and the Catholic communities have illegal secret armies fighting a bloody war. On the Catholic side, are the IRA (Irish Republican Army) and

INLA (Irish National Liberation Army). Both these organizations want to achieve a united Ireland by violent means, but they are condemned today by the government of the Irish Republic. On the Protestant side are the UDA (Ulster Defence Association) and the UVF (Ulster Volunteer Force).

WRITE

Write a short paragraph about each group below, saying what you know about the people, what they want and what they don't want.
1 Ordinary protestants living in Northern Ireland.
2 Ordinary catholics living in Northern Ireland.
3 Members of the IRA and INLA (catholic secret armies).
4 Members of the UDA and UVF (protestant secret armies).
5 The government of the Irish Republic.
6 The British government.

A soldier of the British army on a Belfast street.

The search for a solution

Since 1969 there have been a number of attempts to find a political solution to the Northern Ireland problem. In 1972 the British Government ended the Stormont Parliament, which had failed to give equal rights to Catholics, and Direct Rule of the province from Westminster was introduced. In 1973 there was an agreement – known as the Sunningdale Agreement – between the British Government, the Catholic Nationalists (who wanted a united Ireland) and *some* Protestant Unionists (who wanted Northern Ireland to stay part of the United Kingdom). Many Unionists, however, were against the agreement, because they thought it gave too much power to the Catholic minority in Ulster, and in May 1974 there was a General Strike by Protestant workers, which led to the breakdown of the agreement.

In 1975 there was another attempt at a political solution – the Constitutional Convention. This was an elected group of Northern Irish people, who were to advise the British Government and give their opinions on plans for political change, but the group did not have any real power and, as there were Catholic Nationalists and Protestant Unionists in the group, they could not agree among themselves, and so this attempt also failed.

For five years, no new political attempts were made. Finally, in 1980, the Irish Government (of Eire) began talks with the British Government. There were many problems along the way, but these talks between the two governments eventually led to the Anglo-Irish Agreement in 1985.

ANSWER

1 What do you know about the Northern Irish Parliament at Stormont, and why did the British Government end it in 1972?
2 Why was there a strike in May 1974?
3 What was the result of the strike in 1974?
4 In what way was the 'Constitutional Convention' (1975) the same as a parliament, and in what way was it different?
5 Why do you think there were no new attempts at a political solution from 1975 to 1980?

Stormont, Belfast.

The Anglo-Irish Agreement

On 15th November 1985, the British and Irish governments made a new political agreement on Northern Ireland. The Anglo-Irish Agreement was signed by the British Prime Minister, Margaret Thatcher, and the Irish Prime Minister, Garret Fitzgerald, at Hillsborough Castle near Belfast.

The Agreement gives the Republic of Ireland a voice in the administration of Northern Ireland, and the Irish Government recognizes that there will only be a united Ireland if a majority of people in Ulster agree to it. In addition, both governments said that the Southern Irish and Northern Irish police forces would work together more closely to try to make the border between the two states more secure. They wanted to stop the IRA from hiding in the Republic after they had committed acts of terrorism in the North. The British Government also hoped it would become easier for them to get suspected terrorists, who were in the Republic of Ireland, sent to Britain for trial.

Although the Agreement was welcomed by all political parties in Britain, and by many other countries with a large Irish immigrant population, such as the United States, it was not popular with everyone in Northern Ireland. The Agreement was rejected by many important leaders of the Protestant community, such as Ian Paisley, leader of the Democratic Unionist Party. He told the British Prime Minister

of his view: 'Ulster is British, Mrs Thatcher, and despite your treachery, will remain so'. The Agreement was also rejected by Gerry Adams, President of Sinn Fein ('Ourselves Alone') – the political party which is closely connected to the IRA. These are extreme opinions, however, and many moderate Catholics and Protestants were prepared to give the Agreement a try.

There have been many problems since 1985. The Protestants in Northern Ireland say that border security has not improved enough and that IRA terrorists are still finding a safe place to hide in the Republic of Ireland. The British Government is angry because, on a couple of occasions, the Irish courts set free suspected terrorists instead of sending them to Britain for trial. The Irish Government and the Catholics in Northern Ireland say that Irish people often do not get a fair trial in British courts. They also accuse the British Government of having a 'shoot-to-kill' policy in Northern Ireland, that is to say that the British Army sometimes does not try hard enough to arrest suspected terrorists, but that they just shoot to kill. The British Government, of course, denies this.

In spite of all the difficulties, however, the Anglo-Irish Agreement still stands and the two governments are still working together towards a solution. Can the 1985 Anglo-Irish Agreement eventually succeed, where so many other attempts have failed? Only time will tell.

TALKING POINT

What do *you* think might be the solution to the Northern Irish problem? Should the British Army leave Northern Ireland? What would happen if it did? Should Northern Ireland be united with the Republic of Ireland? What would happen if it was? Should there be another Northern Irish Parliament? How would the Catholics, who are in a minority, be given some share in the power without losing the support of the Protestant majority? Are there any other solutions?

A Holiday

People reading about the troubles in Northern Ireland or seeing the damage caused by bombs on television, probably imagine that the country is one big battlefield. The opposite is true. Many areas of Northern Ireland are beautiful and peaceful. Let us take a brief tour around Ulster and discover some of its beautiful places.

Because the country is only 5,500 square miles (14,250 sq. km.) in area, you can see most of the main attractions in a week without travelling more than 500 miles (800 km.).

Belfast

Belfast is one of the youngest capital cities in the world and it has grown incredibly fast. Today the city has a population of 400,000, nearly a third of the entire population of Northern Ireland, but in the 17th century it was only a village. Then, during the 19th century, the development of industries like linen, rope-making, engineering, tobacco and the sea-trade doubled the town's size every ten years. The city is well-known for shipbuilding – it was here that the 'Titanic', was built and sent out on her fatal maiden voyage.

Some of the Belfast streets have often been the scenes of violence – street-names such as the Falls Road and Shankill Road are well known throughout Britain because they have been heard so often on the news – but people still live in Belfast, and they can and do go out and enjoy themselves. In spite of the years of trouble, there are many cultural and leisure facilities.

Things to do in Belfast...

Visit an ART GALLERY, step into BELFAST CATHEDRAL, go SOUVENIR HUNTING for fine Irish linen, pottery and hand-cut glass in Belfast's covered arcades. If the sun is shining, drive out to STORMONT, the former Parliament building, and walk through the parklands. Whether it rains or shines try your hand at archery or indoor canoeing in one of the city's excellent LEISURE CENTRES, or visit the ZOO.

In the evening go to the THEATRE, the GRAND OPERA HOUSE or a CONCERT at the Ulster Hall – home of the Ulster Orchestra. And finish up at a MUSICAL PUB where you can find a really friendly atmosphere and enjoy some Irish folk music at the same time.

Things to do in Belfast...

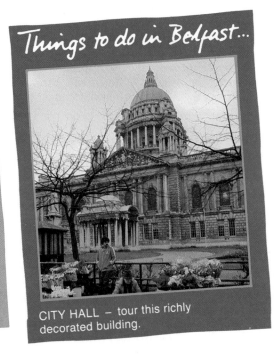

CITY HALL – tour this richly decorated building.

Things to do in Belfast...

ULSTER MUSEUM – see 9,000 years of human history and the gold treasure of the 16th century Spanish war-ship which was recovered off the coast of Antrim in 1968.

Things to do in Belfast...

BOTANIC GARDENS – walk among rare plants and visit the Palm House built in 1850. Some of the tropical plants are 100 years old!

LOOK AND PRACTISE

You and your friend are visiting Northern Ireland and you have one day in Belfast.

Work with a partner. Make suggestions about how to spend the morning, the afternoon and evening. Use the list of 'Things to do in Belfast' to give you ideas, and give reasons for your suggestions and for agreeing or disagreeing to your partner's suggestions. Make a note of your itinerary as you make decisions.

WHY DON'T WE GO TO A MUSICAL PUB?

NO, I DON'T WANT TO.

OH, ALL RIGHT.

I WANT TO GO HOME.

DO YOU FANCY GOING TO VISIT THE ULSTER MUSEUM?

THAT'S A GREAT IDEA.

ACTUALLY I'D RATHER GO SOUVENIR HUNTING.

HOW ABOUT GOING TO AN ART GALLERY?

The Glens of Antrim and the Causeway coast

There are nine glens or valleys of Antrim. Each of these green valleys has a character of its own. Together, they form a lovely and romantic area of rivers, waterfalls, wild flowers and birds.

The people of the Glens are great story-tellers. They will tell you that the places where the little people, or fairies, are said to go, are Lurigethan Mountain and Teveragh Hill. These little people are mischievous and take terrible revenge on anyone who

Peig Sayers: a great story-teller.

cuts down a fairy thorn tree. Today many farmers throughout Ireland are so superstitious that they will not cut down a thorn tree, even if it is in the middle of their field!

The Glens of Antrim were very hard for travellers to reach until the building of the Antrim Coast Road in 1834. For sixty miles this follows the Causeway Coast, named after its most famous feature, the Giant's Causeway.

Stories, legends & myths

Story-telling has always been a part of the Irish way of life – stories of gods and people who lived in a land of adventure, warfare and romance, stories told by the fire side.

Monks living in the late Middle Ages preserved many of these stories in the beautifully-decorated manuscripts of the Book of Leinster. But it is the strong *oral* tradition of the Irish people which has made it possible for so many folk tales to survive. Over the centuries, story-telling was an important profession but nowadays such people would be hard to find. Perhaps the last story-teller was Peig Sayers who died in 1958. It was said that she had 375 stories to tell!

TALKING POINTS

The Irish are said to be a very superstitious race.
- What superstitions are observed in *your* country?
- Are you superstitious?
- Is there any truth in ancient superstitions?

WRITE

Read the legend below about the Giant's Causeway. Then write down a legend or myth of *your* country or local area. If you don't know any legends or myths, make up a story to explain a geographical feature in your country.

The Giant's Causeway – eighth wonder of the world

The Causeway is a mass of stone columns standing very near together. The tops of the columns form stepping stones leading from the cliff foot and disappearing under the sea. Over the whole Causeway there are 40,000 of these stone columns. The tallest are about 42 feet (13 m.) high.

Visitors in modern times have been told that the Causeway is a strange geological feature – the result of volcanic action. The ancient Irish knew differently, however. Clearly, this was giants' work and, in particular, the work of the giant Finn McCool, the Ulster soldier and commander of the armies of the King of All Ireland.

Finn was extremely strong. On one occasion, during a fight with a Scottish giant, he picked up a huge piece of earth and threw it at him.

The earth fell into the Irish Sea and became the Isle of Man. The hole it left filled with water and became the great inland sea of Lough Neagh.

People said that Finn lived on the North Antrim coast and that he fell in love with a lady giant. She lived on an island in the Scottish Hebrides, and so he began to build this wide causeway to bring her across to Ulster.

Irish coffee

Two miles inland from the Giant's Causeway lies Bushmills, the oldest whiskey distillery in the world. Tourists have been stopping here to refresh themselves since 1608!

Ireland is famous for its whiskey which has a taste quite different from Scotch. (Notice that it's spelt differently from Scotch whisky, which has no 'e'.) Here is one well-known way of drinking it.

Pour a measure of Irish Whiskey into a cup of black coffee and sweeten to taste. Pour cream onto the coffee so that it floats on top. (This is best done by pouring the cream carefully over the back of a spoon.) The coffee is then drunk through the cream.

Gaelic names

Years ago, all Irish people spoke Gaelic, and this language is still spoken in some parts of Ireland, although today all Irish people speak English also. Evidence of Gaelic is still found in place names, for example 'bally' – town, 'slieve' – mountain, 'lough' – lake, 'inis' – island, 'drum' – mountain top, 'glen' – valley.

The influence of Irish Gaelic is also found in the names of people. Here are some typical Gaelic first names:

Sean [ʃɔːn], same as John
Seamus ['ʃeiməs], same as James
Liam [liəm], same as William
Seanna ['ʃɔːnə], same as Joanna
Brid [bridʒ], same as Bridget
Catail ['kæhil], same as Charles

Paddy (short for Patrick) and Micky (short for Michael) are not Gaelic names but they are found so often in Ireland that these two names are sometimes used jokingly to mean 'an Irishman'.

Many Irish surnames begin:

O'... meaning from the family of
Fitz... meaning son of
Mc... meaning son of
Kil... meaning son of
Gil... meaning son of

Here are some examples:

O'Brien [əʊ'braiən]
O'Neil [əʊ'niəl]
Kilmartin [kil'maːtn]
Fitzwilliam [fits'wiljəm]
Fitzgerald [fits'dʒerəld]
Gilmurray [gil'mʌri]
McMahon [mək'mæhən]
McHugh [mək'hjuː]

Fermanagh – once fished, never forgotten

Devenish island in Lough Erne.

The rivers and lakes of Fermanagh are heavy with fish, and the largest lake in the area, Lough Erne, holds many world fishing records. Fermanagh is still wonderfully empty of crowds and the fishermen can go all day without meeting anything more than a raven or a swan.

People who don't like fishing can hire a boat on Lough Erne and visit some of the islands in the lake. One of the most interesting islands is Devenish. In the Middle Ages there was a chain of island monasteries in Lough Erne. At Devenish there still stands a perfect 12th century round tower, which the monks used for defence. The island also has a small church of about the same date and the remains of a 15th century abbey.

ASK

Complete this conversation between a local person and a visitor to Fermanagh by asking questions.

1 '...?'
'Well, you can go fishing or take a boat out for the day.'

2 '...?'
'It's excellent, in fact Lough Erne holds some world records.'

3 '...?'
'No, you needn't worry about that. There aren't a lot of tourists around here.'

4 '...?'
'You can visit some of the islands in the lake. In the Middle Ages there used to be monasteries on them.'

5 '...?'
'Well, Devenish is one of the most interesting.'

6 '...?'
'Yes, there's a 12th century round tower and church and the remains of a 15th century abbey.'

Londonderry

The city of Derry has a long history going back fourteen hundred years. At the time of the plantation the City of London in England sent over builders and money to rebuild Derry. As a result, Derry was renamed Londonderry, but today both the long and the short names are used.

The best way to see the city of Derry is to walk along the famous city wall built by the planters in 1614. The wall is about 1 mile (1.5 km.) around and 21 feet (6.5 m.) thick. It is still unbroken – the only complete city wall in Britain or Ireland – in spite of the fact that it has stood against several sieges.

One siege in particular is famous – the Great Siege which started in December 1688 and lasted until July the following year. During this time the city was surrounded by James II's army. 7,000 people out of a population of 30,000 died of starvation before the siege was finally ended. This historical event is still very much alive in people's memories and every year there is a ceremonial closing of the city gates to commemorate the siege.

A tragic story
Near the City of Derry Golf Club, which lies to the north outside the city walls, a family called Knox still lives in a house called Prehen House, where a terrible tragedy took place in 1760.

A local gambler called John Mcnaghten tried to kidnap Mary Ann Knox but she resisted, and during the struggle he accidentally shot her. He was sentenced to death by hanging for the crime, but during the execution the hangman's rope broke. The crowd of people who were watching the execution shouted that he should be saved from the death penalty, since you couldn't hang a man twice. The prisoner, however, shouted that he did not wish to be known as 'half-hanged Mcnaghten', climbed back onto the scaffold and hanged himself!

GAME

Hangman
This game can be played in pairs or in a group. One person thinks of a word and writes down the same number of dashes (lines) as there are letters in the word. For example, if the word thought of is 'SCAFFOLD' (8 letters) he or she would write:

_ _ _ _ _ _ _ _

The other players then suggest letters which might be in the word. Every time a correct letter is chosen it is written in the right place (or places if it comes more than once). Every time a wrong guess is made, a line is drawn to make up a picture of a man being hung, like this:

This drawing is made up of thirteen lines, so the players are allowed twelve wrong guesses before the thirteenth one hangs them, (but eyes, nose, mouth, etc. can be added to increase the number of guesses). Don't forget to keep a record of all wrong letters guessed, so that you don't say the same letter twice.
Good Luck!

Glossary

administration the directing or organizing of affairs in, for example, a business or a country

Anglican Church the Church of England (see pp.7–8)

archery shooting with bows and arrows

border the dividing line between two countries

campaign (*n*) a fight, often used figuratively

causeway raised road especially across wet land

contented happy

county town the chief town of a county

deposed removed from the throne

distillery a place where whiskey is made

force an army

gambler a person who makes a living by games of chance, eg in a casino

geological composition the formation of rocks

glen narrow valley

hostility the feelings of an enemy

house-to-house search looking for someone or something in every house in a particular area

itinerary a journey, route

lasting (*adj*) which continue for a long time

legend an old story

linen fine woven cloth used for bed-sheets, etc.

lough a lake

maiden voyage the first journey of a ship

means ways

myth an old story

Orangemen members of a Protestant political society in Ulster

patron saint a saint regarded as special protector

planter a Protestant settler in Ulster

province one of the main divisions of a country, a separate area for government control (Northern Ireland is often called 'the Province')

put down to defeat

raven a black bird

recover to find, save

rioting a crowd of people causing public disorder

royalist a supporter of the monarchy

sentence to death to punish by death

settler a person who goes to live in a new country

siege (*n*) an attack by an army which surrounds a town and waits for the inhabitants to surrender

sow the seeds to begin something big in a small way

starve to die because of lack of food

stepping stones raised stones in a river

strike a time when workers refuse to work, in protest over something (a **General Strike** is spread over the country, not restricted to just one industry)

in succession one after the other

superstition belief in magic, witchcraft, etc.

suspend to stop for a time

sweeten to taste add as much sugar as you want

terrorism using violence to try to achieve political demands (a **terrorist** is someone who engages in **terrorism**)

treachery disloyalty, falseness, unfaithfulness

try your hand to try something for the first time

world record (*n*) the best yet done in the world

TV and radio

Watching television is one of the great British pastimes! Broadcasting in the United Kingdom is controlled by the British Broadcasting Corporation (BBC) and the Independent Broadcasting Authority (IBA). The BBC receives its income from the government, but the private companies controlled by the IBA earn money from advertising.

National radio is controlled by the BBC, and listeners can choose between four stations. Radio 1 is a pop-music station with news and magazine-style programmes. Radio 2 plays light music and reports on sport. Radio 3 plays classical music whilst Radio 4 has news programmes, drama and general interest programmes. There are many local stations, some private and some run by the BBC. Their programmes consist mainly of music and local news.

The BBC has two TV channels. BBC 2 has more serious programmes and news features. The IBA is responsible for looking after the regional independent TV companies who broadcast their own programmes and those they have bought from other regions. There is a break for advertisements about every 15–20 minutes. The most recent independent channel is called Channel 4 and it has more specialized programmes than the main channels. In general, people think the programmes offered on British television are of a very high standard. Some people, however, are becoming worried about the amount of violence on TV, and the effect this may have on young people.

TV and radio are also two of the main teaching channels used by the Open University. This 'university of the air' allows many thousands of students to study at home for degrees they never would have obtained in the main educational system. They also have to do without sleep as most of their programmes are broadcast early in the morning or late at night!

New technology has made it possible for viewers to receive many more programmes into their homes through satellite TV. The 1990s may well see many changes in British TV and radio.

Top of the Pops

Top of the Pops is a programme that has been shown every week on BBC TV for many years. Each week computers in a number of record-shops throughout the United Kingdom show how many copies of a record have been sold that week. The new chart, issued each Sunday afternoon, shows which singles have sold the most copies during the previous week. With this information, the show's producers decide which songs will be played. Usually it will be those moving up the charts, or the new releases which the disc-jockeys (usually called DJs) think will be 'hits'. Of course, each week the show finishes with the number one single. Bands either appear live in the studio, or in a video recording made especially to sell the record. These videos have become so important in the last few years that they can help to make a record a hit.

More than 30 years of Rock Music

When the American rock-and-roll singer Chuck Berry first sang 'Roll over Beethoven and tell Tchaikowsky the news!' in the 1950s, he was telling the world that the new music, Rock-'n'-Roll, was here to stay. Over the last thirty years it has had an enormous effect on people's lives, and especially on the kind of clothes they wear.

The first group to be seen in the newspapers in the late 50s were the *Teddy Boys*. Their clothes were supposed to be similar to those worn in Edwardian England (Ted and Teddy are abbreviations of Edward): long jackets with velvet collars, drainpipe trousers (so tight they looked like drainpipes!) and brightly-coloured socks. Their shoes had very thick rubber soles and their hair was swept upwards and backwards. Before the arrival of the Teddy Boys young people had usually worn what their parents wore. Now they wore what they liked.

In the mid-60s the *Mods*, (so called because of their 'modern' style of dressing) became the new leaders of teenage fashion. Short hair and smart suits were popular again. But perhaps the Mods' most important possessions were their scooters, usually decorated with large numbers of lights and mirrors. They wore long green anoraks, called parkas, to protect their clothes.

The Mods' greatest enemies were the *Rockers* who despised the Mods' scooters and smart clothes. Like the Teds, Rockers listened mainly to rock-and-roll and had no time for Mod bands such as The Who or the Small Faces. They rode powerful motor-bikes, had long untidy hair, and wore thick leather jackets. Whereas the Mods used purple-hearts (a stimulant or amphetamine, so called because of its colour and shape) 'to get their kicks', the rockers mainly drank alcohol.

In and out of school   127

Throughout the 60s, on public holidays during the summer, groups of Mods and Rockers used to travel to the sea-side resorts of south-eastern England, such as Brighton and Margate, and get involved in battles with the police and with each other.

Nevertheless at that time 'swinging London' was everybody's idea of heaven! Young people were very clothes-conscious and London's Carnaby Street became the fashion centre of Europe and the world. It attracted thousands of tourists every year.

Towards the end of the 60s a new group appeared, whose ideas started in California, in the USA. The *Hippies* preached a philosophy of peace and love, wore necklaces of coloured beads, and gave flowers to surprised strangers on the street. The name comes from the fact that drug-takers in Asia and the Far East used to lie on one hip while smoking opium. Hippies didn't use opium but they smoked marijuana, and took powerful drugs such as LSD. Music, especially under the influence of the Beatles, began to include strange sounds and images in an attempt to recreate the 'psychedelic' or dream-like experience of drugs.

Hippies wore simple clothes, blue jeans and open sandals, and grew their hair very long. They often lived together in large communities, sharing their possessions. This was their protest against the materialism of the 60s and also against the increasing military involvement of the United States in Vietnam.

TALKING POINTS

- Many people use drugs or stimulants in their everyday lives, although they are not usually thought to be as strong or dangerous as the ones mentioned in the text. Make a note of any you can think of.
- What is your attitude to drugs and stimulants? Should we learn to live without them? Should alcohol and cigarettes be banned, since we know they cause so much damage?

However, the dreams of peace and love disappeared in the early 70s as the mood of society changed. People's attention turned to life's more basic problems as the world price of oil increased, causing a fall in living standards and rising inflation.

Skinheads were racist, violent, and proud of the fact. The 'uniform' worn by most of them consisted of trousers that were too short, enormous boots, and braces. As their name suggests, they wore their hair extremely short or even shaved it all off. As unemployment grew throughout the 70s, groups of skinheads began to take their revenge on immigrants, who were attacked on the streets and in their homes.

Unfortunately the mass unemployment of the 80s has caused an increase in the number of skinheads. Many are members of the National Front, a political party that wants Britain to be for white people only.

A skinhead.

Towards the end of the 70s another style of music and dress appeared and is still very popular. The word *Punk* derives from American English and is often used to describe someone who is immoral or worthless. The best-known punk band of the 70s and early 80s were the 'Sex Pistols', who are still famous for their strange names, including Johnny Rotten and Sid Vicious. They sang songs about anarchy and destruction and upset many people by using bad language on television and by insulting the Queen. Punks' clothes show a rejection of conventional styles of dress.

Their music is loud, fast and tuneless. They feel that the music of the 70s had become too complicated. It had lost touch with the feelings of 'ordinary kids'.

In the 1980s many new bands have emerged; and also old ones have

A punk.

reappeared. Out of punk has come *New Wave* music which totally rejects the ideas of the skinheads. Many of the bands contain both black and white musicians, and anti-racism concerts have been organized (known as Rock against Racism). West Indian music has also played a large part in forming people's musical tastes. Many new British bands combine

traditional rock music with an infectious reggae beat. From America, a new interest in discotheques and dancing has appeared.

Like the Rockers, *Bikers* still enjoy 'heavy metal music' which is easily recognized by its high volume and use of electric guitars. 'Dancing' is simply shaking your head violently to the rhythm of the music and so has become known as 'head banging'.

Many of the new bands of the 80s have been able to use the changes in technology to develop their music. Computerized drum machines, synthesizers and other electronic instruments are now just as popular as the electric guitar.

Black music has become increasingly important with international stars like Michael Jackson combining the best of modern music with spectacular live performances. 'Hip Hop' music has combined fast speaking in rhyme (called 'rapping') with the excitement of the rock beat. Finally, Live Aid and charity records have shown that many modern pop stars are interested in using their talents to help raise money for the poor.

READ AND NOTE

The text discusses seven major groups and the music they like: Teddy Boys, Rockers, Mods, Hippies, Punks, Skinheads and Bikers. Write down what you know about each of these groups.

Sport

Sport plays such a large part in British life that many idioms in the English language have come from the world of sport, for example 'to play the game' means 'to be fair', and 'that's not cricket' means 'that's not fair'.

The most popular sport in Britain as a whole is football. A lot of people support their local clubs at matches on Saturday afternoons, or watch the matches live on television.

The football league in England and Wales has four divisions. (Scotland has its own separate system, and there are not many professional sides in Northern Ireland.) Each division contains twenty teams, and at the end of each season the top three clubs from the lower divisions are promoted to a higher one. Those who are at the bottom are relegated. There are two main prizes each season. The football league championship is won by the team that is top of the first division, whereas the FA cup (FA stands for Football Association) is a knockout competition between all the teams of the league. The final of this competition takes place every May at the famous Wembley stadium in London. Some of the best-known clubs in England are Manchester United, Liverpool and the Arsenal. In Scotland either Rangers, Celtic or Aberdeen usually win the cup or the championship.

Many clubs have problems with money at the moment; increasing costs and falling attendances. Some people say that the league is too big and that the players get paid too much. Others say that television is making the crowds stay at home. Many clubs, however, are now earning extra income by using the players' shirts for advertising as a way of staying alive in the 1990s.

Sport at school

Sport has for a long time been a very important part of a child's education in Britain, not just – as you may think – to develop physical abilities, but also to provide a certain kind of moral education! Team games in particular encourage such social qualities as enthusiasm, cooperation, loyalty, unselfishness. Above all, absolute fairness (no cheating!) and being able to lose without anger (being a 'good loser') are considered important.

READ AND PUZZLE

Can you match the pictures of six popular team games in British schools with the six written descriptions?

a A game like the American game of baseball. Played with a long bat held in one hand. The person batting hits the ball and then tries to reach first, second, third or last post before the other team gets the ball back again.

b The scoring of this game is a mystery even to many British people. Each team takes it in turns to bat. The bat is held with both hands, the bottom of the bat resting on the ground. The other team bowls and gets the ball back. Players usually wear white clothes.

c Played with a large leather ball. Each team tries to score goals by throwing the ball through the other team's net.

d Perhaps the most popular game in the world, played in many streets as well as on the field.

e The goalposts in this game are in the shape of the letter 'H'. The ball looks as though someone has sat on it. There is a lot of pushing!

f Each player has a stick with which to hit the ball. This game is played on a pitch similar to a football pitch. The ball is small and hard.

(You will find the answers on page 139.)

The education system

Education in Britain is provided by the Local Education Authority (LEA) in each county. It is financed partly by the Government and partly by local taxes. Until recently, planning and organization were not controlled by central government. Each LEA was free to decide how to organize education in its own area. In September 1988, however, the 'National Curriculum' was introduced, which means that there is now greater governmental control over what is taught in schools.

Nursery education (under 5 years)
Children do not have to go to school until they reach the age of five, but there is some free nursery-school education before that age.

However, LEAs do not have nursery-school places for all who would like them and these places are usually given to families in special circumstances, for example families with one parent only. Because of the small number of nursery schools, parents in many areas have formed play groups where children under 5 years can go for a morning or afternoon a couple of times a week.

Primary education (5 to 11 years)
Primary education takes place in infant schools (pupils aged from 5 to 7 years) and junior schools (from 8 to 11 years). (Some LEAs have a different system in which middle schools replace junior schools and take pupils aged from 9 to 12 years.)

Private education (5 to 18 years)
Some parents choose to pay for private education in spite of the existence of free state education. Private schools are called by different names to state schools: the preparatory (often called 'prep') schools are for pupils aged up to 13, and the public schools are for 13 to 18 year-olds. These schools are very expensive and they are attended by about 5 per cent of the school population.

Secondary education (11 to 16/18 years)
Since the 1944 Education Act of Parliament, free secondary education has been available to all children in Britain. Indeed, children must go to school until the age of 16, and pupils may stay on for one or two years more if they wish.

Secondary schools are usually much larger than primary schools and most children – over 80 per cent – go to a comprehensive school at the age of 11. These schools are not selective – you don't have to pass an exam to go there.

In 1965 the Labour Government introduced the policy of comprehensive education. Before that time, all children took an exam at the age of 11 called the '11+'. Approximately the top 20 per cent were chosen to go to the academic grammar schools. Those who failed the '11+' (80 per cent) went to secondary modern schools.

A lot of people thought that this system of selection at the age of 11 was unfair on many children. So comprehensive schools were introduced to offer suitable courses for pupils of *all* abilities. Some LEAs started to change over to comprehensive education immediately, but some were harder to convince and slower to act. There are a few LEAs who still keep the old system of grammar schools, but most LEAs have now changed over completely to non-selective education in comprehensive schools.

Eton College is probably the most famous public (i.e. private) school in the world. This boy is wearing the school uniform.

prehensive schools

prehensive schools want to develop the talents of each individual child. So they offer a wide choice of subjects, from art and craft, woodwork and domestic science to the sciences, modern languages, computer studies, etc. All these subjects are enjoyed by both girls and boys.

Pupils at comprehensive schools are quite often put into 'sets' for the more academic subjects such as mathematics or languages. Sets are formed according to ability in each subject, so that for example the children in the highest set for maths will not necessarily be in the highest set for French. All pupils move to the next class automatically at the end of the year.

WRITE

Lynn Faulkner is in the Lower Sixth of a comprehensive school. Here she writes about a typical day in her school.

Write a similar account of a typical day in your school. (What tense will you use most?)

My School

A typical day at school starts at 8.40 a.m., with the first of the many bells ringing throughout the building. Pupils must then go to registration, which lasts until 9 o'clock.

After registration, lessons begin. Sixth form pupils must attend the subject lessons that they choose, either at 'O' level or 'A' level standard. My first lesson on a Wednesday morning is English. During this lesson, we usually read a set 'A' level textbook, and then comment and discuss the language and style. After this I have two free study-periods.

The courses chosen by sixth formers are all mixed, and occupy different amounts of time every week. Therefore students usually have a number of periods in which they may study privately. After my two free periods, I have three lessons of Geography, one before morning break, and two afterwards. During break, pupils may buy drinks, sweets, and crisps from the school tuck-shop.

For lunch, many pupils bring sandwiches, but hot and cold meals are available in the school canteen. At 1.15 on Wednesday, school band practice is held. It is quite a big band with about thirty members.

Lessons recommence at two o'clock. Most Lower Sixth pupils have social education on a Wednesday afternoon, which is held in the library, and taken by the head-master. This lesson lasts until quarter past three — the end of school.

School uniform

The pupils at Lynn Faulkner's school, like the pupils at most secondary schools in Britain, have to wear a school uniform. This usually means a white blouse for girls (perhaps with a tie), with a dark-coloured skirt and pullover. The colours may be grey, brown, navy blue, dark green or similar. Boys wear a shirt and tie, dark trousers and dark-coloured pullovers. Pupils of both sexes wear blazers – a kind of jacket – with the school badge on the pocket. They often have to wear some kind of hat on the way to and from school – caps for the boys, and berets or some other kind of hat for the girls. Shoes are usually black or brown and should be sensible – no high heels!

Young people in Britain often don't like their school uniform, especially the hats and shoes. Sometimes they do not wear the right clothes. Schools will often give them a warning the first time that this happens but will then punish them if they continue not to wear the correct uniform.

TALKING POINTS

- Do you think secondary education should be selective or comprehensive? What are the advantages and disadvantages of both systems?
- What do you think are the advantages of school uniform? And the disadvantages?

Computers

Computers have also started to play an important part in education. Most schools in the United Kingdom now have their own computer. As well as using them for school exercises, many young people are now able to write their own games as well. Although a large number of teachers and parents see the advantages of computers, others are not so keen. They say that some young people use computers only for games and don't really learn anything. This will interfere with reading development or traditional hobbies, such as drama or sport. In fact some people say that as computers become better at understanding and speaking we will prefer them to our friends!

TALKING POINTS

- Do you think that some people play computer games too much and too often?
- Do you think that computers could replace teachers in schools? Why?
- What are the advantages and disadvantages of computers? How will they affect your life in the future?

Computer words

The arrival of computers has brought many new words into the English language. How many of these do you know?

WORD-PROCESSOR
HARDWARE
HANDS ON
LAP-TOP COMPUTER
GRAPHICS
ELECTRONIC MAIL
512K
LOADING
MONITOR
DISC DRIVE

wordprocessor = programme to assist in the typing and editing of text before it is printed; hardware = the computer equipment, compare software meaning the programmes themselves; hands on = direct experience of using the computer keyboard, often used now to compare practical experience with theory; lap-top computer = computer that can now be used anywhere, on your 'lap'; graphics = illustrations on a monitor; electronic mail = communications sent from one computer to another down the telephone lines; 512K = 512 kilobytes, computer's memory capacity; loading = transferring information from disc to computer memory; monitor = television that provides visual information from the computer; disc drive = part of computer that operates discs.

Educational reform

In the late 1980s the Conservative Government made important changes to the British educational system. One of the most fundamental changes was the introduction of a new 'National Curriculum'. The aim was to provide a more balanced education.

In secondary schools, for example, 80% of the timetable must be spent on the 'core curriculum'. This must include English, Mathematics, Science and a Modern Language for all pupils up to the age of 16. (Before 1989 pupils of 13 or 14 used to choose the subjects they wanted to continue studying.) At the same time, the new curriculum places greater emphasis on the more practical aspects of education. Skills are being taught which students will need for life and work, and 'work experience' – when pupils who are soon going to leave school spend some time in a business or industry – has become a standard part of the school programme.

Together with the 'National Curriculum', a programme of 'Records of Achievement' was introduced. This programme is known as 'REACH', and it attempts to set learning objectives for each term and year in primary school, and for each component of each subject at secondary school. This has introduced much more central control and standardization into what is taught. Many people think this will raise educational standards, but some teachers argue that they have lost the ability to respond to the needs and interests of *their* pupils, which may be different from pupils in other areas.

As part of the 'REACH' programme, new tests have been introduced for pupils at the ages of 7, 11, 13 and 16. The aim of these tests is to discover any schools or areas which are not teaching to high enough standards. But many parents and teachers are unhappy. They feel that it is a return to the days of the '11+' and that the tests are unfair because they reflect differences in home background rather than in ability. Some teachers also fear that because of preparation for the tests, lessons will be more 'narrow', with a lot of time being spent on Mathematics and English, for example, while other interesting subjects which are not tested may be left out.

Educational reform is bringing other changes too. City Technology Colleges (CTCs) are new super-schools for scientifically gifted children, who – the Government hopes – will be the scientists and technological experts of the future. These schools are partly funded by industry.

In addition to the CTCs, since 1988 the Government has given ordinary schools the right to 'opt out of' (choose to leave) the LEA if a majority of parents want it. Previously all state schools were under the control of the LEA, which provided the schools in its area with money for books etc., paid the teachers, and controlled educational policy. Now schools which opt out will receive money direct from the Government and will be free to spend it as they like. They can even pay teachers more or less than in LEA schools if they want to, and they can accept any children – the pupils do not have to come from the neighbourhood. Many people fear that this will mean a return to selection, i.e. these schools will choose the brightest children. The Government says that the new schools will mean more choice for parents.

Exams

At the age of 14 or 15, in the third or fourth form of secondary school, pupils

PUZZLE

Find the eleven words in the puzzle. They all appear in the 'Educational Reform' section above, and the first letters are given.

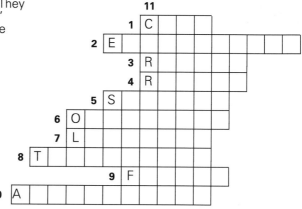

Clues

1 The central part, also the middle of an apple
2 & 3 Changes in schooling, a good title?
4 Written information about past facts
5 An important school subject, Greek knowledge?
6 Goal, aim
7 What people speak if they're modern?
8 Practical science, another modern subject?
9 What education is about, not the present or the past
10 Something that has been successfully done
11 A progamme of study

(You will find the answers on page 139.)

---

begin to choose their exam subjects. In 1988 a new public examination – the General Certificate of Secondary Education (GCSE) – was introduced for 16 year-olds. This examination assesses pupils on the work they do in the 4th and 5th year at secondary school, and is often internally assessed, although there may also be an exam at the end of the course.

Pupils who stay on into the sixth form or who go on to a Sixth Form College (17 year-olds in the Lower Sixth and 18 year-olds in the Upper Sixth) usually fall into two categories. Some pupils will be retaking GCSEs in order to get better grades. Others will study two or three subjects for an 'A' Level (Advanced Level) GCE exam (General Certificate of Education). This is a highly specialized exam and is necessary for University entrance. Since 1988 there has been a new level of exam: the 'AS' Level (Advanced Supplementary), which is worth half an 'A' Level. This means that if pupils wish to study more than two or three subjects in the sixth form they can take a combination of 'A' and 'AS' Levels. In Scotland the exam system is slightly different (see page 90).

Leaving school at sixteen

Many people decide to leave school at the age of 16 and go to a Further Education (FE) College. Here most of the courses are linked to some kind of practical vocational training, for example in engineering, typing, cooking or hairdressing. Some young people are given 'day release' (their employer allows them time off work) so that they can follow a course to help them in their job.

For those 16 year-olds who leave school and who cannot find work but do not want to go to FE College, the Government has introduced the Youth Opportunities Scheme (YOPS). This scheme places young, unemployed people with a business or an industry for six months so that they can get experience of work, and pays them a small wage. They generally have a better chance of getting a job afterwards, and sometimes the company they are placed with offers them a permanent job.

Life at college

British universities

There are 46 universities in Britain. Good 'A' Level results in at least two subjects are necessary to get a place at one. However, good exam passes alone are not enough. Universities choose their students after interviews, and competition for places at university is fierce.

For all British citizens a place at university brings with it a grant from their Local Education authority. The grants cover tuition fees and some of the living expenses. The amount depends on the parents' income. If the parents do not earn much money, their children will receive a full grant which will cover all their expenses.

Free at last!

Most 18 and 19 year-olds in Britain are fairly independent people, and when the time comes to pick a college they usually choose one as far away from home as possible! So, many students in northern and Scottish universities come from the south of England and vice versa. It is very unusual for university students to live at home. Although parents may be a little sad to see this happen, they usually approve of the move, and see it as a necessary part of becoming an adult.

Anyway, the three university terms are only ten weeks each, and during vacation times families are reunited.

Freshers

When they first arrive at college, first year university students are called 'freshers'. A fresher's life can be exciting but terrifying for the first week.

Often freshers will live in a Hall of Residence on or near the college campus, although they may move out into a rented room in their second or third year, or share a house with friends. Many freshers will feel very homesick for the first week or so, but living in hall soon helps them to make new friends.

During the first week, all the clubs and societies hold a 'freshers' fair' during which they try to persuade the new students to join their society. The freshers are told that it is important for them to come into contact with many opinions and activities during their time at university, but the choice can be a bit overwhelming!

On the day that lectures start, groups of freshers are often seen walking around huge campuses, maps in hand and a worried look on their faces. They are learning how difficult it is to change from a school community to one of many thousands. They also learn a new way of studying. As well as lectures, there are regular seminars, at which one of a small group of students (probably not more than ten) reads a paper he or she has written. The paper is then discussed by the tutor and the rest of the group. Once or twice a term, students will have a tutorial. This means that they see a tutor alone to discuss their work and their progress. In Oxford and Cambridge, and some other universities, the study system is based entirely around such tutorials which take place once a week. Attending lectures is optional for 'Oxbridge' students!

After three or four years (depending on the type of course and the university) these students will take their finals. Most of them (over 90 per cent) will get a first, second or third class degree and be able to put BA (Bachelor of Arts) or BSc (Bachelor of Science) after their name. It will have been well earned!

TALKING POINTS

- Is it a good thing to leave home at the age of 18? What are the advantages and disadvantages?
- Many British people believe that if you do nothing more than study hard at university, you will have wasted a great opportunity. What do they mean and do you agree?
- How do British universities differ from universities in your country? What do you like and dislike about the British system?

Glossary

amphetamine a drug which gives a sense of excitement

anarchy when there is confusion in society and no government

anorak a jacket with a hood

badge a special mark, a sign of membership: each school has its own badge

bat (*v*) to hit (especially in cricket or baseball); (*n*) instrument for hitting a ball

beret a soft flat hat for schoolgirls

blazer a jacket

bowl (*v*) to throw a ball

braces elasticated straps which go over the shoulders to keep up one's trousers

break a pause for rest between lessons, usually about 20 minutes

campus the site of a university or college

canteen the place in a school or factory where you can buy food

cap a soft flat hat for men and boys

chart a list of best-selling single records

clothes conscious very aware of the way one dresses

comprehensive (school) providing all types of secondary education

day release the system where someone with a job studies for one day a week

degree a university qualification

disc-jockey a person who plays records on the radio or at a discotheque

division a part of the football league, containing 22 teams

domestic science cookery and housekeeping

do without to survive without something

drainpipe long metal pipe for carrying away water

drug (*n*) a chemical which affects your mind or body

emerge to appear

extracurricular not part of the school timetable

finals final exams at university or college

football season the time of year when football is played, winter in the UK

form (*n*) class

Further Education College college where one can study after the age of 16

get one's kicks to find excitement

grammar school a secondary school which teaches mainly academic subjects

grant money given by an organization, eg the Local Authority

hall of residence a building owned by a college or university, containing study bedrooms for students

here to stay here for ever

hit a successful record

infant school for pupils aged 5–7

infectious (a rhythm) which makes you want to dance

inflation a rise in prices caused by increased wages, etc.

junior school for pupils aged 8–11

keen enthusiastic

knockout a competition which teams leave when beaten

league a group of football teams which play matches among themselves

live (*adj*) not recorded

Local Education Authority (LEA) the education department of local government

lose touch to lose contact

LSD hallucinatory drug (lysergic acid diethylamide)

materialism the belief that you can be happy through the possession of objects

middle school for pupils aged 9–12

moral education learning what is good and bad behaviour

new release a new record

nursery school for children under 5

optional not obligatory

packed lunch a lunch brought from home

paper a piece of writing on an academic subject

pick (*v*) to choose

post (*n*) a piece of wood in the ground

preparatory school a private school for pupils aged 7–13

producer the person who is responsible for a TV or radio programme

public school a private school for pupils aged 13–18

racism belief that your race is superior to all others

registration a period when pupils answer to their names to see if anyone is absent

relegate to send down

rent (*v*) to hire a room for money

resort a place where tourists go to, usually at the seaside

secondary school for pupils aged 11–16/18
selective school a school which pupils must pass certain exams to enter
seminar a discussion
set (*n*) a group of pupils who form a class in a particular subject
set text a literary work which must be studied for an exam
social education lessons to prepare for adult life, not for exams, eg how to manage money, politics

study periods free lessons when pupils can study privately
swinging full of life, sexually free
tuck-shop a place in a school where pupils buy snacks, sweets
tuition fee teaching costs
tutor a teacher in a college or university who leads a discussion group
vice versa the other way round
woodwork the art of making things out of wood

Answers

Quiz (page 14)
1 Anne Boleyn.
2 The Angles.
3 It goes to the House of Lords to be debated.
4 In Scotland.
5 Easter eggs.
6 Ben Nevis.
7 London and the Heart of England.
8 The 'pilgrim fathers' sailed to America in the 'Mayflower'.
9 Seventeen.
10 Five years.
11 People send each other Valentine cards.
12 Upright red cross, white diagonal cross, red diagonal cross.
13 Northern Ireland.
14 On Christmas morning.
15 Because in an election, the wishes of those who voted for the unsuccessful candidates are not represented. The MP who wins an election may have more votes against him than for him.
16 Wales.

Festival crossword (page 14)
Across: 1 ghosts 5 or 6 King 9 penny
           10 in 11 November
Down: 2 home 3 turkey 4 sing 7 noise
         8 on 9 pan

Quiz (page 20)
1 True (The *Financial Times*).
2 Henry VIII.
3 Tower Bridge divides in half to allow ships through.
4 The marriage of Charles, Prince of Wales, and Lady Diana Spencer.
5 London Bridge.

Puzzle (page 21)
1 Barnet Fair: Hair.   4 Plates of meat: Feet.
2 Bees and honey: Money. 5 North and South: Mouth.
3 Daisy roots: Boots.   6 Dog and bone: Telephone.

(guv = governor (boss); butcher's (hook) = look; toad = road; mince pies = eyes)

How much do you remember? (page 26)
Income tax: the Chanellor of the Exchequer/the Treasury
The army: the Ministry of Defence/the Ministry of Defence
Prisons: the Home Secretary/the Home Office
Government spending: the Chancellor of the Exchequer/the Treasury
Law and order: the Home Secretary/the Home Office
Nuclear weapons: the Minister of Defence/the Ministry of Defence
Immigration: the Home Secretary/the Home Office
The police: the Home Secretary/the Home Office

Word Search (page 27)
1 Prince. 2 King. 3 Crown. 4 Royal. 5 Palace.

Quiz (page 34)
1 British Broadcasting Corporation.
2 British Rail.
3 Bachelor of Arts.
4 Member of Parliament.
5 United Nations.
6 European Economic Community.

Word Search (page 45)
1 Swan.   6 Drain.
2 Flat.   7 Island(s).
3 Fen.   8 Tiger.
4 Flood.   9 Celery.
5 Bank.   10 Web.

Look and Practise (page 60)
 1 an Englishman/Englishwoman
 2 a Scot
 3 an Irishman/Irishwoman
 4 a Dubliner
 5 a Greek
 6 a Spaniard
 7 a Dutchman/Dutchwoman
 8 a Frenchman/Frenchwoman
 9 a Londoner
10 a Russian/a Soviet

Complete (page 66)
1 sisters
2 surname, *or* family name
3 parsonage
4 1800
5 novels, *or* stories
6 wrote
7 examples
8 works, *or* books
9 young
10 married

Puzzle (page 87)
1 bed 2 natural 4 living 5 fault 6 picked
7 cabin 8 smoking 9 drilling

True or False? (page 87)
1T 2F 3T 4T 5F 6F 7F 8F

Words (page 89)
1 captain 2 yacht 3 sailing 4 harbour
5 quay 6 ocean 7 river 8 cargo

Quiz (page 90)
1 Voltor 2 Bell 3 Benz 4 Celsius 5 Whittle

Words (page 101)
Boys' names
Thomas, Ian, Michael, Kenneth, James, Robert,
Andrew, Mark, Martin, Frederick.

Girls' names
Ruth, Julia, Gemma, Tracy, Teresa, Angela, Marilyn,
April, Felicity, Gillian.

Surnames
Thomas, Smith, Rogers, Abbot, James, Robinson, Price,
MacGregor, Peters.

Mixed names
Elizabeth, Nigel, George, Susan, Angela, Robert, Diana,
Monica, Peter.

Write (page 105)
Order of sentences: 2, 4, 7, 3, 1, 8, 5, 6

Word Game (page 106)
1 Welsh 2 New Theatre 3 Attractive
4 Administrative 5 Steel 6 Evening 7 Study

Word Search (page 108)
Sailing, Singing, Theatre, Climbing, Riding, Rugby

True or False (page 109)
1T 2F 3T 4F 5T 6F 7T

Puzzle (page 114)
1 population   4 plantation
2 colonization   5 reformation
3 industrialization   6 starvation

Read and Puzzle (page 130)
a rounders   d football
b cricket   e rugby
c netball   f hockey

Puzzle (page 135)
1 core 2/3 educational reform 4 record
5 science 6 objective 7 language 8 technology
9 future 10 achievement

Index